TABLE OF CONTENTS *(cont.)*

INTRODUCTION

Schools are moving into the Information Age, and the computer is becoming an essential classroom tool and resource. Successful students in the 21st century will need the abilities to think critically, engage in problem solving, and possess interpersonal skills to work effectively in cooperative groups. In addition, they will need to be highly literate and know how to use technology to access and organize information.

Integrating Technology into the Math Curriculum (Primary) is a 144-page resource book that provides strategies and activities for integrating technology skills into the grades 1–3 math curriculum. These integrated lessons allow teachers to incorporate computer work into their existing curriculum. After all, what teacher has the time available in the instructional day to add a new subject area? Not only would this be difficult, if not impossible, it would not be in the best interest of students. Research shows that an integrated curriculum is much more valuable. Therefore, the foundation for this book, infusing technology skills into the curriculum, is a more meaningful approach to teaching and learning.

The activities in this book are designed to incorporate computer technology into the math curriculum with such transparency that the focus remains on the math concept. The technology is simply another tool to be used in conveying the ideas of mathematical principles in such a way that young minds can easily grasp them. Just as counting teddy bears or unifix cubes helps students visualize number combinations, exploring the "virtual manipulatives" on a computer screen helps to bring mathematical ideas from the abstract to the concrete.

Watch for the Software Connection following many of the lessons in this book. These special pages identify a popular piece of software that has "pre-packaged" activities that can be used to readily convey the concept addressed in the lesson. These titles take away the prep time involved in creating the lesson template and offer one simple solution specific to the theme. Additionally, the activities cited are self-adjusting to offer easier problems to the novice, and more challenging problems to the advanced student. What better way to individualize instruction!

Prior to the lessons, *Integrating Technology into the Math Curriculum (Primary)* provides information on managing computers in the classroom, whether it be a one-computer classroom, multi-computer classroom, or lab setting. It also includes realistic ways to group students for instruction and practice, as well as positive ways to manage behavior. In addition, successful tips for writing and obtaining grants are discussed.

Enjoy!

Contributing Editors:
Amy Seely Flint, Ph.D.
Nancy Casolaro

Project Manager:
Betsy Morris, Ph.D.

Editor in Chief:
Sharon Coan, M.S. Ed.

Art Director:
Elayne Roberts

Art Coordinator Assistant:
Cheri Macoubrie Wilson

Cover Artist:
Tina DeLeon

Product Manager:
Phil Garcia

Imaging:
Ralph Olmedo Jr.

Acknowledgements:
Mighty Math Zoo Zillions and *Carnival Countdown* software and screen shots (pages 20, 25, 30, 34, 38, 39, 42, 46, 53, 57, 113, 114) are ©1997 Edmark and used by permission.

Kid Pix 2®, Copyright Brøderbund Software, Inc., 1996. All Rights Reserved.

The Cruncher, courtesy of Davidson & Associates, Inc. ©1994 Davidson & Associates, Inc. All rights reserved.

Publishers:
Rachelle Cracchiolo, M.S. Ed.
Mary Dupuy Smith, M.S. Ed.

INTEGRATING TECHNOLOGY
into the
Math
Curriculum

PRIMARY

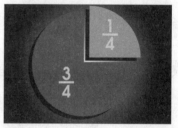

Author:
Deborah Hamill

Teacher Created Materials, Inc.
6421 Industry Way
Westminster, CA 92683
ISBN-1-57690-424-5

©1999 Teacher Created Materials, Inc.   Made in U.S.A.

TABLE OF CONTENTS

THE ONE-COMPUTER CLASSROOM

The one-computer classroom is a challenge for the teacher, but with some planning and thought it is manageable. While lessons can take longer to complete, sometimes days longer than with the use of a lab, teachers in one-computer classrooms can still provide their students with meaningful and enjoyable computer experiences.

Some questions arise when considering the logistics of a one-computer classroom. For example,

- What will the other students do when not on the computer?
- How will the teacher assess each child's progress?
- What kind of system will allow each child a turn?

While these questions are not anything new to teachers, the computer does present some unique situations.

Getting Started

Students will have to be shown how to perform certain operations. These are directions of a physical nature and at times will need to be step-by-step. This means the teacher may have to spend time with individual students until they learn how to click the mouse, click on buttons, or drag and drop objects on the screen. Some planning will be required to ensure that the teacher can work with one or two students while the rest of the class has another task.

An equitable system for students to have time to work on assignments must be planned as well. One of the best methods is to rotate students on a daily basis to do assigned tasks. If a projection device is available, the whole class can work together on some things.

Projection Devices

Projection devices can be expensive but are worth the investment. Since a projection device is not something that teachers use every day, it might be more feasible if several teachers in a school request one that could be shared. A projection device allows the teacher to show the whole class the computer screen at the same time and introduce new material on the computer efficiently with one computer. Students will still need some hands-on time when learning new skills, but with a projection device, the learning curve will be much shorter. Also, many of the lessons in this book can become whole-class activities, especially when introduced or reviewed by using a projection device.

There are several types of projection devices, and they come in a wide range of prices. LCD (liquid crystal display) panels are among the most affordable. They generally start around $1,500 for one with good resolution. They can go up to more than $5,000 for deluxe models. Regardless of the model, LCD panels are simple to use; they fit on top of an overhead projector and connect to the computer. The overhead projects what is on the computer through the LCD panel to a screen in the front of the room. It is important to have an overhead projector that lights up from the base so that its light travels through the LCD panel. Most overheads sold today are made to do this. Older overhead projectors may have their light source in the head that is above the base. This type of overhead will not work with an LCD panel.

THE ONE-COMPUTER CLASSROOM (cont.)

Another popular type of projection device is a television that is modified with a translator card and a special cord so that it can translate the computer's digital signal into an analog signal that can be shown by the television. This type of projection device usually costs less than an LCD panel but does not offer the clarity of picture or resolution found with LCD panels.

Projectors are one-piece devices that connect to the computer and then directly project onto the screen. They offer the best looking picture around, but they are also the most costly. Projectors usually start around $5,000.

When looking for the best price, it is best to look in several catalogs. Check with area computer stores and the school librarian for catalogs that feature projection devices. These devices are becoming more affordable as they become more available.

If the computer has not yet been purchased, try to get an oversized monitor and arrange it so that so that the monitor is slightly raised. This will allow a group of students to view the monitor as they sit around the computer table. While this solution is not a projection system, it will help make things a little easier when the teacher is working with a small group around the computer.

Whole-Class Instruction

There are many activities in this book that begin or follow up with a class discussion. As teachers, we know that a great deal can be accomplished by talking with students and modeling the appropriate behavior or skill. Therefore, regardless of the number of computers in the classroom, teachers must utilize traditional intructional practices when teaching technology skills.

Teachers will need to spend time teaching basic skills to students in the beginning, but once students learn these skills, they will become more independent, freeing the teacher to work in other areas of the classroom. Students who use the computer regularly and see teachers using it regularly will develop a higher level of computer literacy, and more quickly, than students who rarely use or see one used.

THE ONE-COMPUTER CLASSROOM *(cont.)*

There are lessons in this resource book that do not even involve the use of a computer, because a lot of the curriculum for computers at the primary level involves teaching students the vocabulary of computers. This means giving them activities that promote intuitive understanding of what the terminology means. Students need to know what is actually happening when they use database software to sort or order records. With intuitive understanding of the functions, they will be able to interpret and use the results of the computer's response more effectively. Lessons like these help young students develop an understanding of computer functions and commands. This helps them become computer literate much faster when they are introduced to more complex software, such as spreadsheets, in the later grades.

Making It Work

Using the computer, talking about the computer, and exploring what can be done with the computer will go a long way toward satisfying almost any primary technology curriculum. It will also provide a sound understanding of the basics of daily computer work that will help students to advance in both technical skills and understanding of concepts as they proceed through the grades.

Teachers do not need a lot of peripherals or a huge computer lab to teach technology skills. One computer with a paint program, multimedia software, and an integrated office package that provides database, spreadsheet, and word processing applications can be the basis for satisfying both the curriculum's technology objectives and the students' needs for the future.

THE MULTI-COMPUTER CLASSROOM

The multi-computer classroom has three or more computers and allows the teacher to work with small groups or the entire class in technology-based activities and to use the computers in many different ways simultaneously.

Grouping Students

In a multi-computer classroom it is necessary to organize the students into cooperative groups so that they can get the most out of computer time. A group of students can be assigned to each computer, where they can research, create projects, publish writing, and save their work. It is important that students are grouped with different abilities, genders, and technology competencies. Also, groups should be switched periodically to provide the students opportunities to work with others in the classroom.

Each member within a group needs to be assigned a specific task for the duration of each activity. These tasks can be put on laminated cards, and students can choose a task card before an activity begins. There are many tasks that can be performed by students. (The teacher should determine which ones are appropriate for each lesson.) Some examples of tasks for computer-based activities are

- Recorder—records group's data
- Cleaner—puts supplies away
- Tracker—makes sure that group members stay on task
- Supplier—gets supplies for group
- Presenter—presents group's findings to class
- Text Writer—inputs text into the computer
- Graphics Artist—inputs graphics items into the computer
- Calculator—performs calculations on the computer
- Graph Maker—makes the computer graph

THE MULTI-COMPUTER CLASSROOM *(cont.)*

It is important to have special rules that apply when students are working in cooperative groups. Each group can make a short list of rules that they will follow when they are working together. Or, perhaps more appropriate for younger children, the teacher can hold a class discussion and decide the special rules that will be needed for group work. Regardless of the method used to determine the rules, they should be written down for all to see. Older students can write the rules on on a piece of paper along with the name of the group's project and each group member's name and assigned task. This piece of paper can be attached to a pocket folder in which each group keeps a disk and all written work related to the project.

Noise Level Control

Many of the activities in the multi-computer classroom are cooperative-learning based. In this environment, the students are encouraged to communicate with each other. A classroom of 25 students can create a lot of noise when they are working on a project. Therefore, it is necessary to have a system of controlling noise. An example that works well is a numerical system, where the 0 signifies "Silence;" a 1 "Quiet;" a 2 "Conversation;" and a 3 "Presentation."

0	Silence	
1	Quiet	☺
2	Conversation	☺ ☺
3	Presentation	☺ ☺ ☺

Laminated cards can be displayed at each computer or in the front of the classroom to indicate the accepted noise level for an activity.

At times, it may be necessary to get everyone's attention quickly. A signal for complete silence could simply be to turn off the classroom lights. This signal tells the students to stop whatever they are doing, look at the teacher, and listen for directions.

THE MULTI-COMPUTER CLASSROOM *(cont.)*

Asking for Help

When working in cooperative groups, students will have questions that many times can be answered by other group members. In fact, it is valuable to teach students other ways of finding answers, besides asking the teacher. For those questions that must be answered by the teacher, one idea is to have students place a brightly colored plastic cup on top of the computer monitor to signal that help is needed.

Equity

Making sure that all students have an opportunity to work on the computer can be difficult. Teachers can make this task easier if they use a visual display to indicate who has or has not been to the computer. There are a variety of ways to record this, but one simple way is to place a laminated square near each computer. Divide the square in half. The left side of the square is designated for those students who have not been to the computer, and the right side is for those students who have.

At the beginning of the week, place a clothespin for each group member on the "Not Been There Yet" side of the square. As the students participate in computer activities, they move their clothespins from the "Not Been There Yet" to the "Been There, Done That" side. When everyone in the group has had a turn, the clothespins are put on the "Not Been There Yet" side of the square again.

THE MULTI-COMPUTER CLASSROOM *(cont.)*

Behavior Management

Due to the nature of the cooperative learning environment, teachers must have clear expectations and specific guidelines for acceptable student behavior in the multi-computer classroom. The teacher may want students to do some role playing exercises to reinforce acceptable classroom behavior. Students can help in generating these rules. The teacher may even want students to participate in choosing logical consequences for poor behavior choices. Below are some rules that are appropriate for a primary multi-computer classroom.

RULES

1. Enter quietly and ready to listen.
2. Respect your work and the work of others.
3. Treat the equipment with respect.
4. Listen carefully and follow directions.
5. Clean up your area and exit quietly

Computer Journals

It is helpful for each student to keep a computer journal. Students can make entries in their journals at the end of each activity. They can explain what they have learned about the subject, describe what they did on the computer, and list any problems they had using the computer or working within their group. The teacher should review the journals to track student progress, address student problems, and evaluate what the students have learned during each activity.

THE COMPUTER LAB

The ideal situation for schools is to have a computer lab equipped with enough computers for every student in a class, as well as computers in each classroom for students to work on when not in the lab. The downfall of a lab setting is that students only visit it periodically (perhaps once a week) and thereby lose practice and daily experiences with technology. Therefore, having a few computers in each classroom, in addition to a school lab, is the most beneficial for all.

Lab Schedules

In most schools with a lab setting, each class is assigned one class period per week to work in the computer lab. Teachers may decide that for one week one teacher will bring both classes to the computer lab and vice versa. This allows each classroom teacher the option of either teaching the lesson, having the paired teacher teach it for both classes, or having the technology lab specialist teach the lesson (if one is available).

An important thing to remember is that activities in the computer lab must be curriculum related. The lab should not be free time to play games or just draw pictures! Students should be given instruction and work on an activity or project that relates to what they are studying in class.

It is helpful when scheduling lab lessons to leave a regular block of time or day of the week when the lab is free. That way, teachers can schedule an extra period for the entire class or group of students. (This is particularly helpful when long-term projects are being developed.)

Assigned Seats

A seating chart is extremely important for the lab setting, as students are in a different setting and tend to become excited and therefore noisy. A permanent, assigned seat will help students focus on the task at hand and realize that the goal is to work in the lab, not to socialize with friends.

COMPUTER LAB SCHEDULE

Monday May 4, 1998

Time	Teacher	Subject	Objective	Software	Technology Specialist Needed for
8:05–9:00	Teacher A			___ ClarisWorks ___ Kid Pix 2 ___ SuperPrint ___ HyperStudio ___ Internet ___ Other	___ Instruction ___ Support ___ Home
9:00–9:45	Teacher B			___ ClarisWorks ___ Kid Pix 2 ___ SuperPrint ___ HyperStudio ___ Internet ___ Other	___ Instruction ___ Support ___ Home
9:45–10:30	Teacher C			___ ClarisWorks ___ Kid Pix 2 ___ SuperPrint ___ HyperStudio ___ Internet ___ Other	___ Instruction ___ Support ___ Home
10:30–11:15	Teacher D			___ ClarisWorks ___ Kid Pix 2 ___ SuperPrint ___ HyperStudio ___ Internet ___ Other	___ Instruction ___ Support ___ Home
11:15–12:00	Teacher E			___ ClarisWorks ___ Kid Pix 2 ___ SuperPrint ___ HyperStudio ___ Internet ___ Other	___ Instruction ___ Support ___ Home
12:00–12:45	Teacher F			___ ClarisWorks ___ Kid Pix 2 ___ SuperPrint ___ HyperStudio ___ Internet ___ Other	___ Instruction ___ Support ___ Home
12:45–1:30	Teacher G			___ ClarisWorks ___ Kid Pix 2 ___ SuperPrint ___ HyperStudio ___ Internet ___ Other	___ Instruction ___ Support ___ Home
1:30–2:15	Teacher H			___ ClarisWorks ___ Kid Pix 2 ___ SuperPrint ___ HyperStudio ___ Internet ___ Other	___ Instruction ___ Support ___ Home

COMPUTER LAB LAYOUT

Even Printer

Odd Printer

Large Screen Monitor

Teacher's Desk

Teacher's Name

Door

WRITING A GRANT

Writing A Grant

Everyone uses technology, right? Well, no. There are great differences in the number of computers and the capabilities of computers at schools throughout the country. Some schools are equipped with a full computer lab of 30 up-to-the-minute computers, many color printers, scanners, digital cameras, LCD panels for viewing—-you name it! These schools might also have several computer stations in each classroom, again fully equipped. On the other end of the spectrum are schools that might have a computer station available for two or three classrooms to share. How do the fortunate schools acquire computer equipment? Much of it is purchased outright with PTA support or help from business/school partnerships. Some of it is donated by local organizations. While these are all good sources, the possibility of acquiring hardware, software, and peripherals through grants should not be overlooked.

Many schools create grant writing teams. These teams often include teachers, parents, and administrators who come together to write proposals for possible funding from various sources. A team propvides the opportunity to brainstorm good ideas with others and divide the work. Grant writing can be a time consuming task.

Who?

Begin with your school district. Many districts give small grants to teachers or teams of teachers for specific needs. They may offer stipends for projects developed that will enhance teaching and learning. Usually, these projects need to help more than one class and can be replicated and made available to other teachers.

Next, seek out a community foundation which funds projects just in your county. Often an RFP (request for proposal) is accepted quarterly or annually, depending on the foundation or corporation. Corporations continually offer funding as a way to publicly support education as well as receive a tax write off for the company.

The government at federal, state, and local levels have many grant opportunities available, some more well-known than others. Seek out these possibilities aggressively. The money is there, and your school might as well be the recipient.

WRITING A GRANT *(cont.)*

Where?

To locate grant funding sources, start with your local library or the Internet. The library has indices to help identify the most appropriate grant for your situation. The Internet has search tools that simplify the job immensely. A tip when searching the Internet is to be specific in the use of keywords. Try entering *grants + technology* to connect two words in your search term. Here are a few sources available on the Internet to get you started:

U.S. Department of Education
(see Money Matters)
http://www.ed.gov

Grants Web
http://web.fie.com/ews/sra/resource.htm

Council on Foundations
http://www.cof.org

Fedworld Information Network
http://www.fedworld.gov

Grant Writer Online
http://www.grantwriteronline.com

Prove It

Those who review grant proposals want hard evidence that you will attempt to measure the outcome of the plan. Include proof that technology can help solve the problem. For example, state that seventy percent of the third-grade students will show at least a four-point improvement in their reading scores. The entire faculty will receive staff development training in the use of the hardware and software necessary to achieve these goals.

Determine a Time Line

Tell how long the project will take. For instance, "staff development will begin in September and be successfully completed in eight weeks. Students will begin work at multimedia work stations by November, and their slide shows will be completed by February. They will share their slide shows with parents at an open house and with other classrooms after the PTA Open House. These students will then become tutors for students the following year."

Research the Budget

It is extremely important to itemize absolutely everything you need for the project, including personnel for training, stipends for staff development, and all hardware and software. This is where you demonstrate the research that goes into your grant. If continuing funds are necessary, you need to stipulate where you will get those funds.

WRITING A GRANT *(cont.)*

How?

It takes some thought and practice to match the project with the right funding source. You will need to carefully read the RFP (request for proposal) and follow all instructions exactly. If others in your district have responded to RFPs previously, you may want to use their documents as a model. Check with your district office to see what is available before "reinventing the wheel."

Success!

It is very unusual for a first-time grant writer to achieve success. Don't become discouraged. A "no" may really mean "not at this time." If you are fortunate enough to meet success the first time, you will most likely be energized to try for an even bigger grant. If you were told that your grant was a good one but not selected at this time, try again with a different funder. Look over the RFP carefully, and submit it again. Go back to your team for more brainstorming. Perhaps your budget needs review, or maybe some items can be eliminated or postponed for later.

For further information on grant writing, see Teacher Created Materials' *Writing Grants* by Julia Jasmine.

Good luck ... there's lots of money out there. Go get it!

EVEN OR ODD?

Drag and match sets of objects on the computer to determine whether a number is even or odd.

Grade Level: 1–2

Duration: 15–20 minutes at the computer

Materials: Computer with paint software; paint file on page 19

Before the computer:

- The teacher should introduce the concept of even and odd numbers to students by pairing up various objects in the classroom: if every object has a mate, then the number is even; if there is an object without a mate, then the number is odd.

- The teacher should create and save the paint file on page 19.

- Students should know how to drag and drop objects on the screen and how to print.

At the computer:

- Display the paint file on the monitor.

- Show students the first problem and tell them that this activity will help them learn how to tell even numbers from odd numbers.

- Demonstrate to students how to drag the objects into two lines to pair them up.

- Ask students if all the objects have a partner.

- Remind students that if all the objects in the group have a partner, the number is even. If a block in the group is left by itself, the number is odd.

- Ask students to tell you if the number is even or odd based on this criteria.

- Allow students to complete the activity independently on the computer.

- After lining up the objects into pairs, have students type the number of objects with an "E" or "O" beside it.

- Ask students to print the page.

- Tell students to close the file and not save the changes. This will return the file to its original state for others to use.

Extensions:

- Add more numbers to figure out whether they are odd or even.

- Stamps can be used instead of blocks to compliment subjects, holidays, or themes.

- Students can create their own problems for other students to solve.

EVEN OR ODD? *(cont.)*

EVEN OR ODD? *(cont.)*

SOFTWARE CONNECTION:

Suggested software: *Zoo Zillions* by Edmark

There is a good practice and review section for even and odd numbers in the "Annie's Jungle Trail" module of this math and problem-solving software for Kindergarten, First, and Second grades.

From the opening screen, go to Annie's Jungle Trail. Click on the grow bar icon in the bottom left corner of the screen. Click on Topics in the dialogue box. Select letter I (Odd or Even), and click OK.

This activity can be played by one or two players, or in teams. The activity asks students to identify whether a number is even or odd. If a student identifies an even number as odd, the crocodile moderator reminds the student that even numbers must end in 2, 4, 6, 8, or 0.

More advanced students can choose the letter R and identify even or odd 2-digit numbers.

POCKETS, POCKETS, POCKETS

> **Sharpen students' understanding of place value. Place paint objects into digital "pockets."**
>
> **Grade Level:** 1–2
>
> **Duration:** 20–30 minutes at the computer
>
> **Materials:** Computer with paint software; printer; paint file on page 22; copies of pocket activity sheet; construction paper; copies of tens strips and ones blocks activity sheet; white paper; glue; scissors

Before the computer:

- The teacher should create the paint file on page 22. Copies of the activity sheet should be available for each student. Have students cut out the pockets and glue them onto a piece of construction paper. Leave the top of the pocket open for placing objects in the pockets. The pocket labeled "tens" should be on the left; the "ones" on the right.

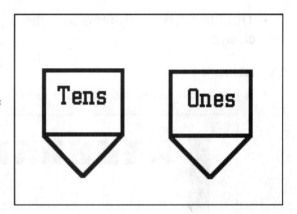

- Have students cut out twenty "ones" blocks and ten "tens" strips from the activity sheet. The teacher should review the concept of tens and ones using manipulative models if desired.

- Students should be familiar with the drag and drop features of the paint program.

At the computer:

- Display the paint file of the pockets on the monitor.

- Explain to students that they are going to place strips and blocks into their "pockets" as you demonstrate it on the computer.

- Choose a two digit number and write it where children can see it easily.

- Ask students how many tens are in this number.

- On the screen, drag the correct number of tens strips to the tens pocket. Have students place the correct number of tens strips into their tens pocket on their activity sheet.

- Ask students how many ones are in this number.

POCKETS, POCKETS, POCKETS *(cont.)*

At the computer: *(cont.)*

- Drag the correct number of ones blocks to the ones pocket on the screen. Have students place the correct amount of ones blocks into the ones pocket on their worksheet.

- Take the strips and blocks out of the pockets on screen. Have students empty their pockets.

- Display the next two digit number where everyone can see it.

- Repeat the process of dragging strips and blocks into the pockets on screen, while students place their strips and blocks into the pockets on their activity sheets.

- Continue this demonstration until students have a good understanding of this process.

- Tell students that they will be able to use the paint file later to complete this activity on the computer.

- This file can be easily restored to the original screen by closing the file without saving any changes.

Extensions:

- A hundreds pocket can be added to the file and activity sheet.

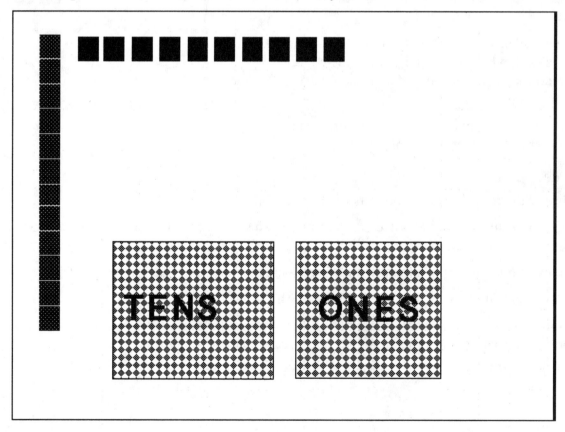

To the teacher:

- Use a paint program to create this file or something similar.

- Other numbers to have children illustrate: 25, 17, 31, 50, 44, 73, 8, 61, 82, 96.

POCKETS, POCKETS, POCKETS *(cont.)*

TENS AND ONES

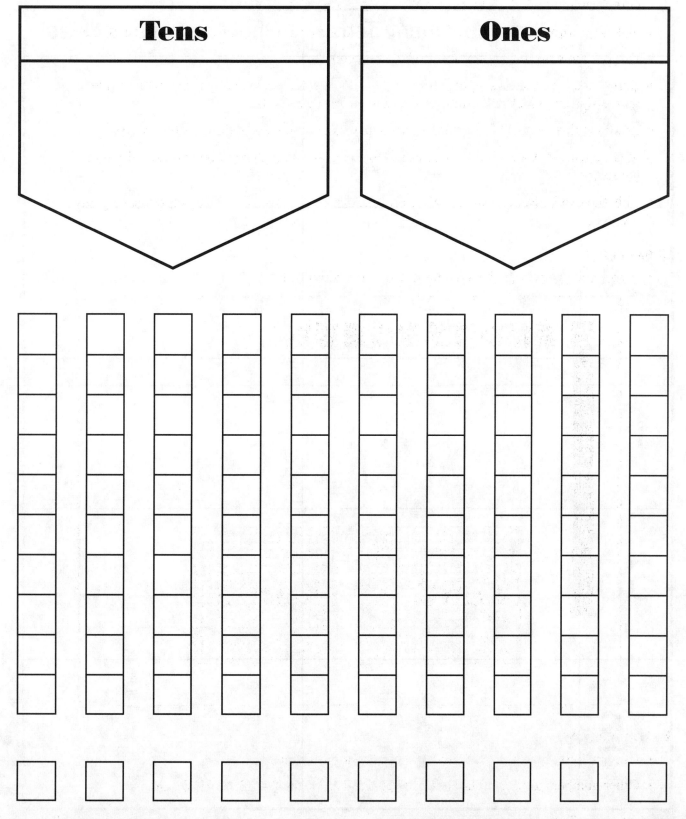

POCKETS, POCKETS, POCKETS *(cont.)*

Name _____

	Show how many Tens	Show how many Ones
34		
24		
17		
56		
72		

POCKETS, POCKETS, POCKETS *(cont.)*

SOFTWARE CONNECTION:

Suggested software: *Carnival Countdown* by Edmark

Students can use the explore mode of Bubble Band to play with the idea of exchanging ones for tens, and tens for hundreds. This module allows children to visualize the concept of place value as numbers are represented by bubbles that can be grouped, manipulated, and exchanged. There is also a question and answer mode where Eddie the moderator entices children to respond to his request for a number of a certain value.

From the opening screen, go to Eddie's Bubble Band. Click on the grow bar icon in the bottom left corner of the screen. Click on Topics in the dialogue box. Select the topic area appropriate for the aptitude of your students. Choices include:

- Numbers Through 19 as Tens and Ones
- Trade 10 Ones for 1 Ten
- Trade 10 Ones for 1 Hundred
- Trade Ones, Tens and Hundreds

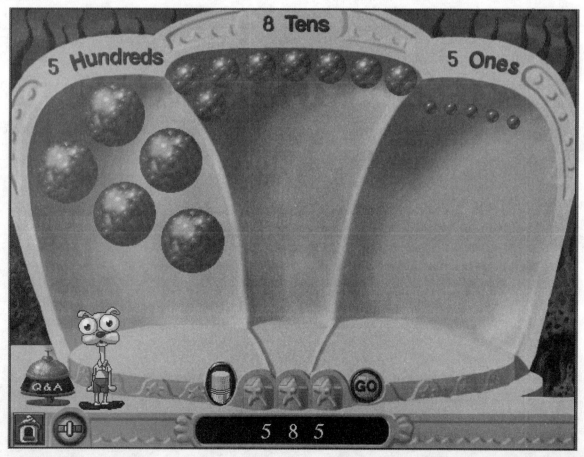

ALIEN NUMBERS

> **Work with the numbers from the planet Juno (an imaginary planet in a galaxy far, far away) to understand place value.**
>
> **Grade Level:** 1–2
>
> **Duration:** 15–20 minutes on the computer
>
> **Materials:** Computer with paint software; printer; paint file on page 27

Before the computer:

- The teacher should create the paint file shown on page 27.

- Students should be familiar with place value for two-digit numbers.

- Students should know how to use the stamp function and the draw and paint tools and understand how to drag and drop objects on the screen.

- Students should also know how to print.

At the computer:

- Display the paint file on the monitor. Explain that many cultures have different number systems. Explain that this number system is from the planet Juno, an imaginary planet in a galaxy far, far away.

- Ask students if they see any similarities between Juno's number system and our number system.

- Ask students how many tens are in the first number. How many tens are in the second number? What do they think represents tens on Juno?

- Ask students to state how many ones are in the first number. How many ones are in the second number? What do they think represents ones on Juno?

- Have students work independently using the stamp feature (or draw tools) to complete the activity.

- Instruct students to print their results.

- Tell students to close the file without saving the changes. This will automatically erase the illustrations and return the file to its original state.

Extensions:

- Three-digit numbers can be used in the file.

- Students can make up their own number system and give it to a friend to translate.

ALIEN NUMBERS

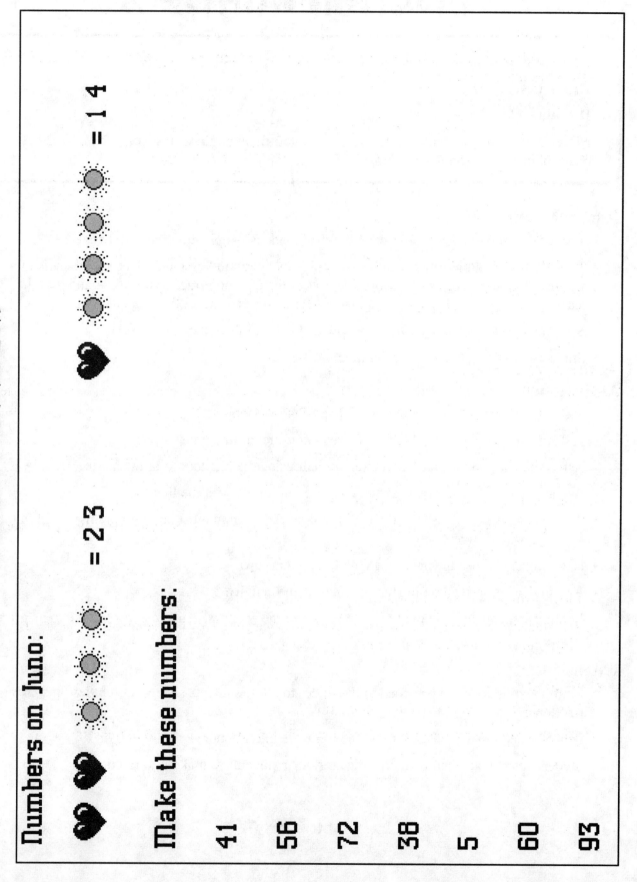

Numbers on Juno:

= 23

= 14

Make these numbers:

41

56

72

38

5

60

93

FRACTION PAINTINGS

Divide pictures into fractional parts.

Grade Level: 1–2

Duration: 15 minutes on the computer

Materials: Computer with paint program; printer; file with drawings shown on page 29; chart models of fractions (optional)

Before the computer:

- The teacher should create and save a file that contains the pictures shown on page 29.

- The teacher should review fractions with students by reminding them that they are parts of a whole. Use chart models of fractions to review the common fractions of $\frac{1}{4}$, $\frac{1}{2}$ and $\frac{1}{3}$. The teacher can also use physical manipulatives for students to make fractions of a whole.

- Students should be familiar with the draw and paint tools in the paint software.

- Students should know how to print their work.

At the computer:

- Display the paint file with pictures of shapes on the monitor.

- Tell students they will divide these shapes into different fractions.

- Ask a student to divide the first picture in half using the line tool to draw the line.

- Ask another student to divide another picture into thirds with the line tool.

- Show students how to use the floodfill (paint bucket icon in most paint programs) to fill in the fractions with different colors.

- Have students finish the pictures in the file on their own.

- Ask students to print the file after completing the activity.

- Remind students to close the file without saving the changes. This restores the file to its original state.

Extensions:

- More painting files can be added to the folder to allow students new opportunities for making fractions.

- Sets of objects can be placed in the file to divide into fractions.

- Students can create their own drawings for other students to make into fractions.

FRACTION PAINTINGS

Name _____

1.   ¹/₂

2.   ¹/₂

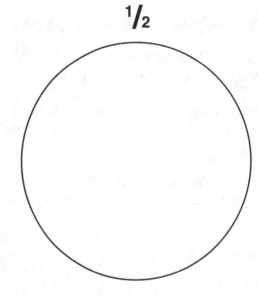

¹/₂

4.

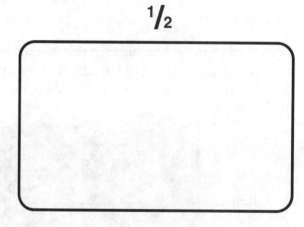

3.   ¹/₂

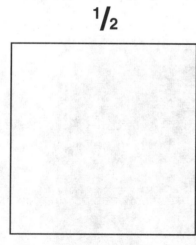

¹/₂

5.

FRACTION PAINTINGS

SOFTWARE CONNECTION:

Suggested software: *Carnival Countdown* by Edmark

"Annie's Pattern Block Roundup" module allows students to demonstrate their knowledge of fractions by responding to Annie's prompts.

From the opening screen, go to Annie's Pattern Block Roundup. Click on the grow bar icon in the bottom left corner of the screen. Click on Topics in the dialogue box. Select $\frac{1}{2}$ of a Shape and click OK.

This activity can be played by one player or two players taking turns. The program shows one shape divided in half and asks students to identify another picture that shows one half of the shape colored in.

For the students ready for a bigger challenge, go to Topics and choose "Identify $\frac{1}{3}$, $\frac{1}{4}$, and $\frac{1}{6}$ of a Shape."

As students demonstrate their understanding of the concept of fractions, the activities become gradually more difficult. If a child misses several in a row, the program automatically steps them back to easier problems.

There is also an explore mode in this module that allows students to build their own shapes using pattern blocks. If desired, students can work in pairs with one student building shapes and challenging the other student to color in a fractional portion of that shape.

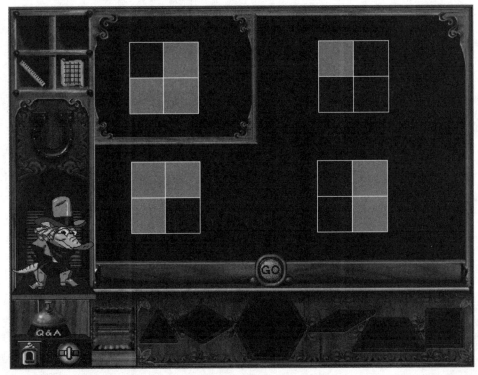

CAN YOU MAKE IT?

Challenge children to follow oral directions.

Grade Level: K–2

Duration: 20–30 minutes at the computer

Materials: Computer with paint software; printer; copies of the activity sheet on page 32; an older student, teacher's aide, or parent volunteer to read the directions

Before using the computer:

- The teacher should make a copy of the activity sheet for each student.

- Students should be familiar with using the paint and draw tools and should know how to print.

- Students should also know how to use the floodfill tool (paint bucket icon on most paint software programs) and be familiar with the stamp function.

At the computer:

- Display a blank screen on the monitor.

- Explain to students that they are going to follow oral directions to create various objects on screen.

- Have an older student, teacher's aide or parent volunteer read the directions to students as they work on the computer.

- Have students use the paint, drawing tools and stamp functions to make the picture.

- Have students print their work to turn in with the activity sheet.

- When everyone has finished, review what items each picture should contain.

Extensions:

- Students can create directions for others to follow.

- The directions can be made longer and more complicated depending on the level of the students.

CAN YOU MAKE IT? *(cont.)*

Name _____

Follow these steps:

Draw a big circle and color it blue.

Draw 5 pumpkins inside the circle.

Draw 3 birds outside the circle.

Draw a big rectangle and color it green.

Draw 4 animals inside the rectangle.

Draw 10 flowers outside the square.

Erase 2 pumpkins.

Erase 1 flower.

Add 2 bugs inside the circle.

Add 2 + 1 houses inside the square.

Print your picture.

CAN YOU MAKE IT? *(cont.)*

 ## SOFTWARE CONNECTION:

Suggested software: *Zoo Zillions* by Edmark

A variation on this activity can be done using the 3D Gallery module in *Zoo Zillions* product. The emphasis would be on recognizing geometric shapes and following oral directions. Less time would be spent on the drawing process if it was decided to use the pre-existing shapes in this software product, anad more time would be spent on spatial visualization skills and vocabulary building.

The teacher should prepare a set of instructions for the child to follow to build a design. If the directions are printed out in rebus style using pictures of the geometric shapes, some children might be at a reading level where they could complete this exercise on their own by following the written instructions. For other children, the teacher might consider reading the instructions into a tape recorder that the children can pause after completing each instruction, and create their design step by step. Or the teacher can use classroom volunteers to read the directions aloud to non-readers.

This is a good opportunity to use peer tutoring, perhaps bringing older children into the classroom to read the instructions and then critique the finished design to see if it meets the oral directions given.

Working, independently or in pairs, students can create their own directions for a partner to follow in constructing animals or objects from oral instructions. Or, students can work individually in the Question and Answer mode. Here the Otter Twins display a picture made of 3D geometric objects and ask the student to identify a particular shape that is part of the object by clicking on that shape. The Otter Twins act as coaches when needed to offer hints and help the student identify the correct shape.

As in all modules of the Edmark Mighty Math series, the student can click on the Grow Slide button to increase the difficulty of the questions or choose a different topic to explore. In this way the program adjusts to the child's ability level and "grows" with the student as he or she masters a particular concept and needs a new challenge.

From the opening screen, go to 3D Gallery. Click on the Q & A bell in the bottom left corner of the screen to toggle between Q & A or Explore mode.

CAN YOU MAKE IT? *(cont.)*

SUBTRACTION ACTION

Create and move pictures to illustrate the various combinations of the number 5.

Grade Level: K–1

Duration: 30 minutes at the computer

Materials: Computer with paint software; printer; copies of the activity sheet on page 37

Before the computer:

- The teacher should make a copy of the activity sheet for each pair of students.

- The teacher should model this activity for the students using the computer, an overhead projector, or the chalkboard.

- Students should be familiar with the stamp function and the draw and paint tools. Students should also know how to print their drawings.

At the computer:

- Display a blank document in the paint software on the monitor.

- Divide students into pairs.

- Explain to students that they will be illustrating number sentences for the number 5 using stamps or the paint and draw tools.

- Tell Student A to stamp 5 copies of a chosen stamp in a row across the top of the screen.

- Student B should drag any subset of those stamps down to the bottom of the page.

- Students should then work together to create a number sentence representing their actions on the activity sheet.

- Students should drag the stamps back to the top of the page so that all 5 are in a row again.

- On the next turn, Student A should drag a different subset of that group down to the bottom of the page.

- Partners work together to record the appropriate number sentence.

- This activity should continue until all possible combinations of the number 5 have been recorded.

- Students should print their pictures to turn in along with the activity sheet.

Extensions:

- Students can illustrate the combinations and write number sentences for other numbers.

SUBTRACTION ACTION *(cont.)*

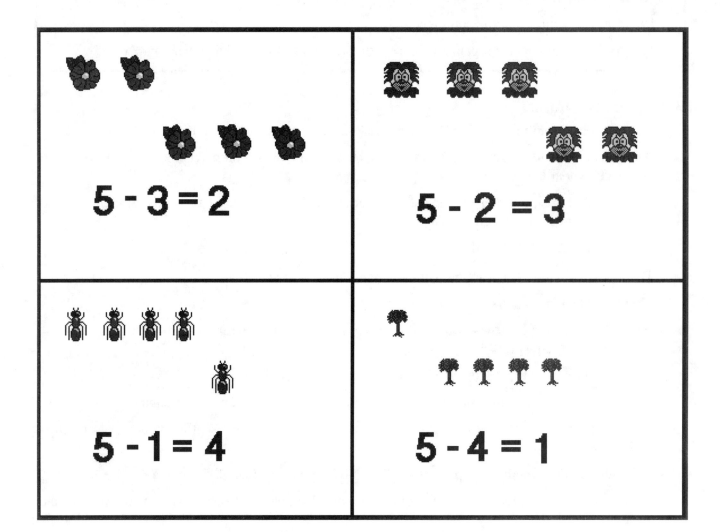

SUBTRACTION ACTION *(cont.)*

Names_____ and _____

Here are the number sentences we found for the number 5:

_____ − _____ = _____

_____ − _____ = _____

_____ − _____ = _____

_____ − _____ = _____

_____ − _____ = _____

_____ − _____ = _____

SUBTRACTION ACTION *(cont.)*

SOFTWARE CONNECTION:

Suggested software: *Carnival Countdown* by Edmark

The "Fish Stories" module allows students to create their own number sentences by manipulating the visuals in the explore mode. They can see their number sentence build as they add or remove fish from the tank, and they can hear the story problem read aloud.

By clicking the + sign, students can create addition problems. By clicking the – sign, students can create subtraction problems.

From the opening screen, click on the fish pond to go to Eddie's Fish Stories. Click on the bell in the bottom left corner of the screen to toggle to the Explore mode.

Students can drag fish in and out of the tank to create addition and subtraction number sentences that illustrate the different combinations that make up the number 5 (or any number you wish for them to concentrate on.)

SUBTRACTION ACTION *(cont.)*

Students see the story problem at the top of the page change to reflect the number of fish in the picture.

They can hear their story read at any time by clicking on the mouth next to the story.

Students create their number sentences by clicking on the numerals at the bottom of the screen.

Students can print their fish stories to have a visual representation of each of the equations that make up the number 5 and create a number 5 storybook.

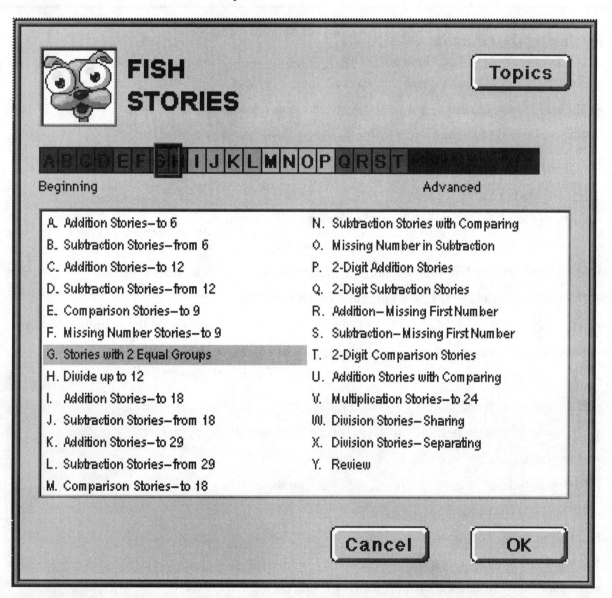

For extended reinforcement of a family of facts, students can toggle back to the Question and Answer mode. Clicking on the "Grow Slide" at the bottom of the screen brings up a number of topics. The teacher can set the activity to give the child practice on a particular topic (i.e., addition problems up to 12). As students demonstrate their understanding of this topic, the questions become gradually more challenging. If a child responds to a question incorrectly, the program reduces the number of possible choices and encourages the student to try again.

ACTING OUT ADDITION

> **Solve addition problems by manipulating objects on screen.**
>
> **Grade Level:** K–1
>
> **Duration:** 15–20 minutes on the computer
>
> **Materials:** Computer with paint software; printer; paint file on page 41; unifix cubes (optional)

Before using the computer:

- The teacher should review the basics of addition, reminding students that addition means putting groups together. Unifix cubes can be used for the review.
- The teacher should create the paint file as shown on page 41.
- Students should be familiar with drag and drop in the paint program.
- Students should also know how to use the text tool in the paint program and how to print.

At the computer:

- Display the addition file in the paint program on the monitor.
- Tell students that they are going to use blocks on the screen to find answers to addition problems.
- Show students the first problem and the groups of blocks beside the problem.
- Demonstrate to students how to drag the blocks into one group.
- Ask a student to count the number of blocks and record the answer on the computer screen.
- Show students the next problem and the groups of blocks beside the problem.
- Ask a student to drag the blocks into one group and then count the number of blocks in the group.
- Have the student record the answer on the screen.
- Give students the opportunity to solve the problems on the computer.
- Have students print their file when finished.
- Remind students to close the file without saving the changes. This restores the file to its original state.

Extensions:

- Students can solve addition problems using 3 numbers.
- Students can create their own problems for others to solve.

ACTING OUT ADDITION *(cont.)*

Acting Out Addition

Name _____

3
+<u>4</u>

5
+<u>6</u>

7
+<u>9</u>

6
+<u>4</u>

5
+<u>7</u>

ACTING OUT ADDITION *(cont.)*

SOFTWARE CONNECTION:

Suggested software: *Carnival Clowns* by Edmark

In the same way that unifix cubes allow children to physically manipulate objects to represent addition, the "Snap Clowns" module of this program allows students to visually manipulate clowns to reinforce the idea that addition means grouping objects.

The added features of being able to see the number sentence change as students add or remove clowns from the pole, along with the ability to hear the numbers spoken aloud, make this module particularly powerful in reinforcing students' understanding of how the grouping of objects relates to numeric symbols.

Students can use the activity sheet developed for this lesson in the Explore Mode of "Snap Clowns."

From the main screen, students click on the picture of the circus tents to go to the "Snap Clowns" module. Clicking on the bell in the lower left corner toggles the program to Explore Mode.

Students can use two poles to represent the addends on the activity sheet.

Snap the correct number of clowns to the first pole to represent the first addend; snap the correct number of clowns to the second pole to represent the 2nd addend.

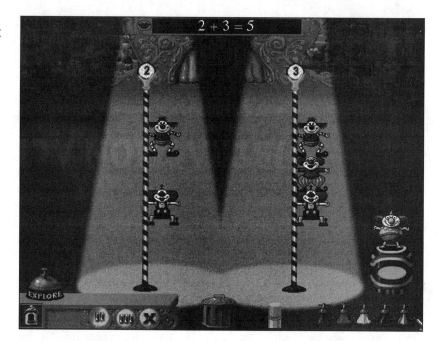

Students count the total number of clowns and write that number on their activity sheets. Or, students can print out their picture of the clowns with the complete number sentence showing at the top of the page.

For added practice, toggle the module back to the Question and Answer mode. Choose the topic appropriate for the focus of the lesson from the "Grow Slide."

MICE IN A HOLE

Hide objects on screen and challenge a friend to guess how many are missing.

Grade Level: K–1

Duration: 20 minutes at the computer

Materials: Computer with paint software; printer; copies of the activity sheet on page 45

Before the computer:

- The teacher should make enough copies of the activity sheets for each pair of students.
- The teacher may want to demonstrate the steps involved in this activity on a large monitor or LCD panel.
- Students should be familiar with the drag and drop features of the paint program.
- Students should know how to draw a circle and how to delete an object.
- Students should be familiar with the print function.

At the computer:

- Begin with a blank document in the paint software.
- Have students work in pairs.
- Let each group chose a background for their picture or create one of their own. See illustration on page 41.
- Student A stamps 7 small mice onto the background.
- Student B points to each object and counts aloud to verify the correct number of mice.
- While Student B looks away or covers his or her eyes, Student A draws a filled circle over one or more of the mice to hide them. See illustration on page 41.
- Student B then looks at the remaining animals and tells how many mice are hiding in the hole.
- Student A deletes the hole to reveal the mice underneath.
- Partners can count together to verify Student B's answer.
- Give each pair of students an activity sheet and have them record their findings. Students should print the screens to turn in with their activity sheets.
- Students then switch roles and repeat the exercise.

Extensions:

- Students can print their drawings and exchange them with other teams, who can write the appropriate number sentences for the illustrated drawings.

MICE IN A HOLE *(cont.)*

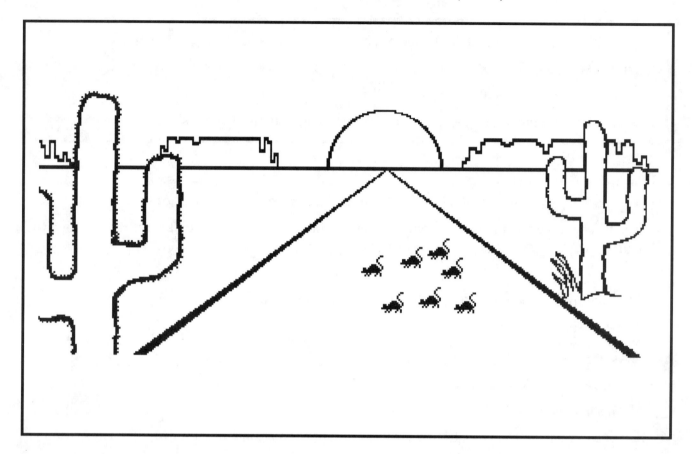

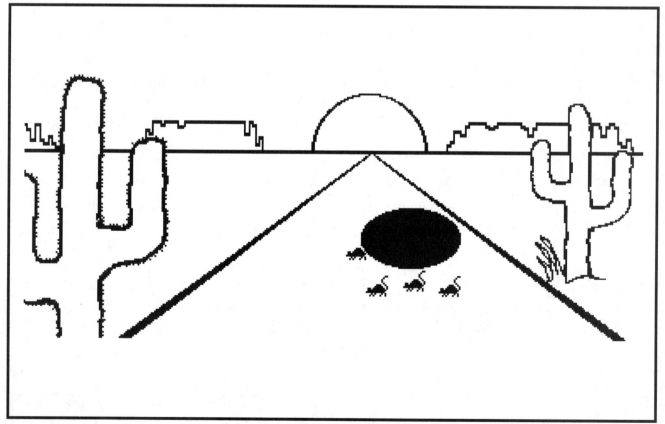

MICE IN A HOLE *(cont.)*

Names _____ and_____

1. How many mice are there to start?_____

   How many are hiding? _____

   How many can you still see on screen? _____

   The number sentence for this is _____ – _____ = _____

2. How many mice are there to start?_____

   How many are hiding? _____

   How many can you still see on screen? _____

   The number sentence for this is _____ – _____ = _____

3. How many mice are there to start?_____

   How many are hiding? _____

   How many can you still see on screen? _____

   The number sentence for this is _____ – _____ = _____

4. How many mice are there to start?_____

   How many are hiding? _____

   How many can you still see on screen? _____

   The number sentence for this is _____ – _____ = _____

5. How many mice are there to start?_____

   How many are hiding? _____

   How many can you still see on screen? _____

   The number sentence for this is _____ – _____ = _____

MICE IN A HOLE *(cont.)*

SOFTWARE CONNECTION:

Suggested software: *Zoo Zillions* by Edmark

This same activity can be performed in the "Fish Stories" module of *Zoo Zillions*.

From the opening screen, click on the fish pond to go to Eddie's Fish Stories.

Click on the "Grow Slide" at the bottom of the screen and click on Topics.

Choose Topic O: Missing number in subtraction (or any of the topics that relate to subtraction).

Students are given a story problem and need to manipulate fish in and out of the tank to fit the story.

They can hear their story read again at any time by clicking on the mouth next to the story.

Then they are asked to build the number sentence that represents their actions.

Students can print their fish stories to have a visual representation of each of the equations, or they can use the activity sheet with this lesson to record their sentences.

SPREADSHEET INVESTIGATION

Solve addition problems with a spreadsheet program.

Grade Level: 1–2

Duration: 20 minutes on the computer

Materials: Computer with spreadsheet software; printer; file with spreadsheet template on page 48; copies of activity sheet on page 49

Before the computer:

- The teacher should create the spreadsheet template as shown on page 48, making sure to include the calculation formulas listed.
- The teacher should also make a copy of the activity sheet for each student.
- The teacher should review the concept of addends with students.
- Students should know how to add information to a document.

At the computer:

- Display the spreadsheet template on the monitor.
- Explain to students that they will be learning how to use a spreadsheet.
- Introduce the spreadsheet format and show students how to enter numbers into cells. Explain that the computer already has been given the command to add the numbers in row 1 and row 2. Show students where to look for the answers.
- Using the first problem on the spreadsheet template, play "what if" with the students. Ask students what they think the answer will be if the missing number is 3.
- After students provide guesses, tell them you want to see what the computer comes up with.
- Have a student enter the number 3 into the missing addend cell on the spreadsheet and let the computer generate the answer.
- Ask students if they were correct in their guesses.
- Continue to play "what if" in this manner until the spreadsheet is completed.
- Tell students that they will have the opportunity to fill in their own spreadsheets with their own missing addends.
- Have students use the activity sheet to play "what if." Have students check their predictions to see if they were correct.
- Tell students to print their spreadsheets and close the file without saving the changes. This restores the spreadsheet to its original state for others to use.
- Students can also use their spreadsheets to play "what if" with a partner. If the answer is ___, then the missing addend is ___.

Extensions:

- Students can use a similar spreadsheet set up for subtraction problems.
- Students can create problems for each other to solve.

SPREADSHEET INVESTIGATION *(cont.)*

	A	B	C	D	E
1	5	3	2	1	6
2					
3					

Notes on constructing Spreadsheet Investigation:

Put the numbers indicated above in row 1.

Row 2 should remain blank.

Row 3 should have the formula for adding row 1 and row 2 together. This will allow students to put different numbers in row 2 and the spreadsheet will automatically calculate the answer in row 3.

Calculation symbols will vary and the manual for your software should be checked for the correct symbols to perform the necessary function. Cells 3B-3E should have a formula that sums (Σ) the two cells above it respectively.

Numbers in cell should be a large point size for easy viewing. At least a 24-point size or larger is best.

SPREADSHEET INVESTIGATION *(cont.)*

Name _____

Record the numbers you plan to put in the spreadsheet. Write the answers you think the computer will give.

Column A

5	5	5	5

Column B

3	3	3	3

Column C

2	2	2	2

Column D

1	1	1	1

Column E

6	6	6	6

BRACELET BEADS

Create friendship bracelets of a certain value.

Grade Level: 1–2

Duration: 15–20 minutes on the computer

Materials: Computer with paint software; printer; paint file on page 51; activity sheet on page 52

Before the computer:

- The teacher should create the paint file as shown on page 51.
- The teacher should make a copy of the activity sheet for each student.
- Students should be familiar with drag and drop in the paint program and the stamp function.
- Students should also know how to use the text tool and how to print.

At the computer:

- Display the paint file on the monitor.
- Tell students that they are going to make friendship bracelets that cost a particular amount of money. Explain that each bead shown is worth a certain amount of money. Tell students they must add beads to determine the value of the bracelet. Explain that each bracelet may have several correct answers.
- Tell students they may wish to connect the beads with a line tool.
- Ask a student to make a bracelet worth 13¢. See if someone else can make it a different way.
- Give students the activity sheet and let them solve the problems on the computer.
- Have students print their work to turn in with the activity sheet.
- Remind students to close the file without saving the changes. This restores the file to its original state.

Extensions:

- More beads worth different amounts can be added.
- Restrictions can be put on the number of beads used.
- Students can be asked for more than one solution to each problem.

BRACELET BEADS *(cont.)*

Directions for creating this file:

Use the stamps to choose beads your students will enjoy.   If you change the beads, adjust the student activity sheet. Use the text tool to label the beads.

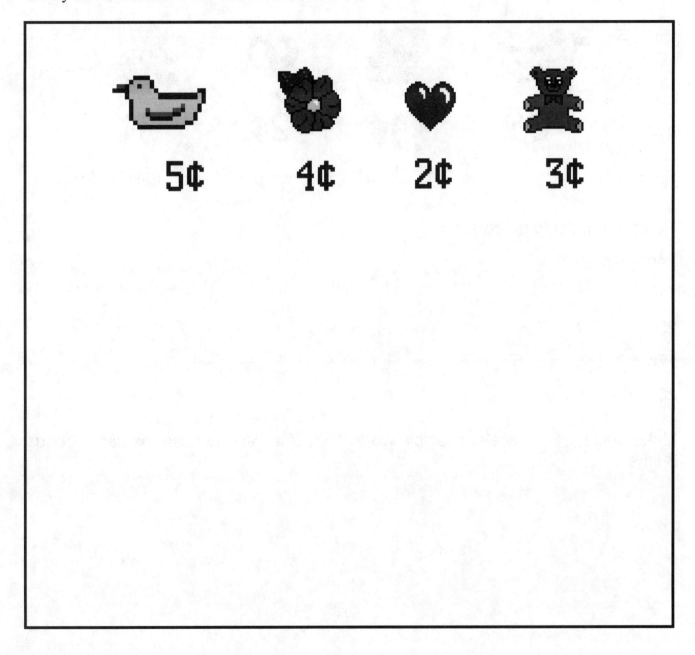

BRACELET BEADS *(cont.)*

Name _____

Use the computer to solve these problems. Print out the answers.

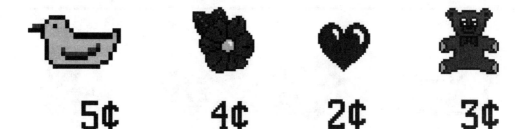

Make a friendship bracelet worth:

24¢

12¢

25¢

17¢

20¢

Make the longest bracelet possible worth 16¢. You can only use the same bead 3 times.

BRACELET BEADS (cont.)

SOFTWARE CONNECTION:

Suggested software: *Zoo Zillions* by Edmark

Students can experience a similar activity in the "Gnu Ewe" module of *Zoo Zillions*.

From the opening screen, click on the cave to go to the Gnu Ewe Boutique.

Click on the "Grow Slide" at the bottom of the screen and click on Topics.

Choose a topic that allows the students to add two and three amounts to 99¢ (or any of the topics for which they need individual practice).

Students are asked to choose items from the boutique to help dress the characters.

Then they are asked to add up the amounts to see the total bill. If children are having trouble, Allison the Elephant helps them by providing hints. If further help is needed, the program automatically starts to eliminate number choices until the child solves the problem correctly.

When the final total is calculated correctly, the character purchasing the items displays the correct amount of cash on the counter. This visually reinvorces money awareness as the child can see the correct coins that add up to the total amount of money needed for the purchase.

Choosing other topics can give the child practice in selecting the right combination of coins for a purchase, making change, finding equivalent sums of money, and various other topics that reinforce the concept of money.

POCKETS OF COINS

Manipulate virtual coins to solve the problems.

Grade Level: 2–3

Duration: 20–30 minutes at the computer

Materials: Computer with paint software; printer; paint file on page 55; copies of the activity sheet on page 56

Before using the computer:

- The teacher should create the paint file as shown on page 55.
- The teacher should make a copy of the activity sheet for each student.
- Students should be familiar with the drag and drop function of the software.
- Students should also know how to print their drawings.

At the computer:

- Display the paint file on the monitor.
- Explain to students that there are story problems involving money on the activity sheet. Tell them that though you can't give every student real coins to work with, you can give them virtual coins to help solve the problems. Tell students they may move the coins up to the top of screen to help figure out the answers.
- Give students copies of the activity sheet and let them work independently at the computer.
- Have students print their work to turn in with the activity sheet.
- Remind students to close the file without saving the changes. This restores the file to its original state.

Extensions:

- Students can create new problems for other students to solve.
- Virtual paper money can be added to the file.

POCKETS OF COINS *(cont.)*

Notes on construction of the paint file:

Use the circle and text tools to create these coins. Leave space at the top of the screen for students to move around money.

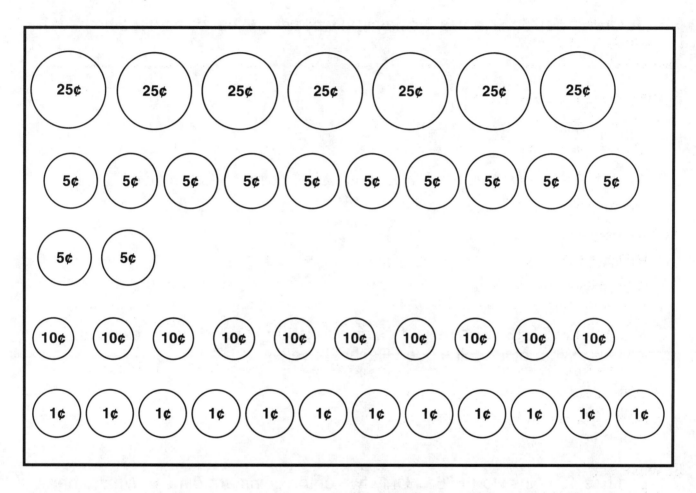

POCKETS OF COINS (cont.)

Name _____

Use the computer to solve these problems. Print your answers.

1. Andrew has 77¢. He has 8 coins in his pocket. What coins does he have?

    quarters

    dimes

    nickels

    pennies

2. Amy has 41¢. What is the fewest number of coins she can have?

    quarters

    dimes

    nickels

    pennies

3. Rachel has $1.43. She has 14 coins altogether. Only 3 of the coins are nickels. What other coins does Rachel have?

    quarters

    dimes

    pennies

4. Jen has 16 coins worth 86¢. Only two of the coins are dimes. What other coins does she have?

    quarters

    nickels

    pennies

5. Rob has 11 coins in his pocket worth 52¢. What coins does he have?

    quarters

    dimes

    nickels

    pennies

POCKETS OF COINS *(cont.)*

SOFTWARE CONNECTION:

Suggested software: *Zoo Zillions* by Edmark

For further practice and review in counting coins, have students visit the Gnu Ewe Boutique in Edmark's *Zoo Zillions*.

From the opening screen, click on the cave to go to the Gnu Ewe Boutique.

Click on the "Grow Slide" at the bottom of the screen and then click on Topics.

Choose one of the several topics that allow the students to count coins (or any of the topics for which they need individual practice).

Students can manipulate virtual coins as Allison the Elephant asks them to make change, find equivalents, and exchange coins for dollar bills.

ADDITION RULES

> **Come up with the solution to these puzzling problems.**
>
> **Grade Level:** 2–3
>
> **Duration:** 20 minutes at the computer.
>
> **Materials:** Computer with multimedia authoring software; printer; multimedia slideshow storyboard on pages 59–60

Before using the computer:

- The teacher should create and save the slideshow storyboard on pages 59–60.
- Students should be familiar with using the slideshow feature of multimedia programs. Students should know how to move from slide to slide and should know how to use the text and delete tools.
- Students should be familiar with the print function.

At the computer:

- Display the slideshow file on the monitor.
- Explain to students that they will be asked to solve a series of puzzles like this one. They must be careful to follow all the rules. They will work on the computer where it will be easier to enter numbers (or to enter dots to count) to solve the problems. If they make a mistake, they can easily change it.
- Have students work on the computer independently to solve these puzzles.
- Ask students to print out their solutions and to print out their new puzzles.
- Display the original puzzles on a bulletin board for others to solve.
- Remind students to close the file without saving the changes so that others may complete the activity.

Extensions:

- Students can create more puzzles in different pattterns.

ADDITION RULES (cont.)

Notes on construction:

Use the shape, line, and text tools of the multimedia slideshow program. Be sure that there is a button on each slide to move to the next slide.

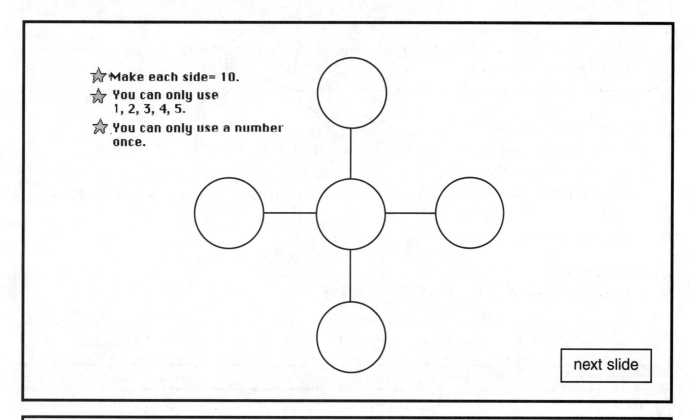

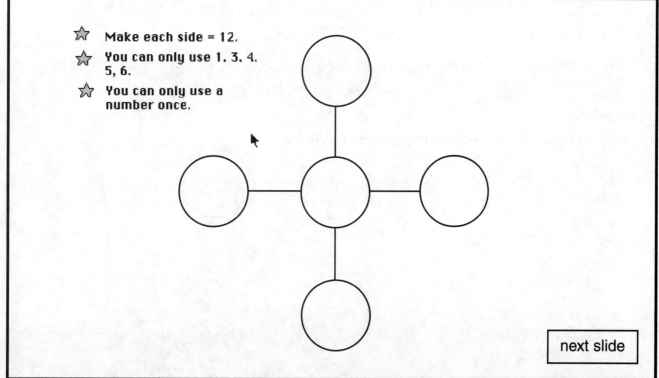

ADDITION RULES *(cont.)*

⭐ **Make each line = 14.**

⭐ **You can use 1, 2, 3, 4, 5, 6, 7, 8.**

⭐ **There is one number you can use twice.**

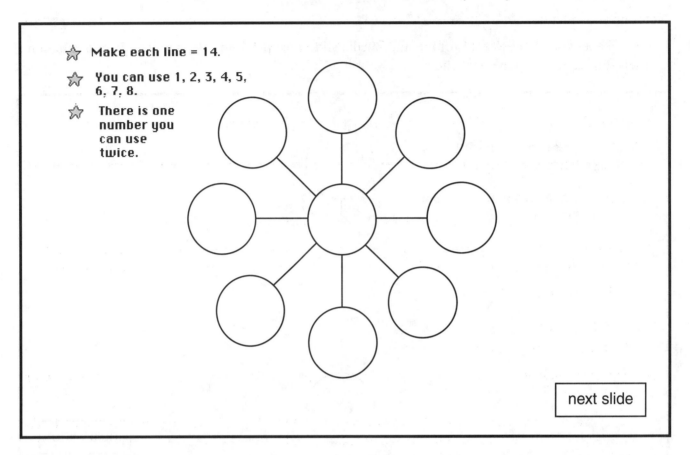

next slide

Make a puzzle for a friend.

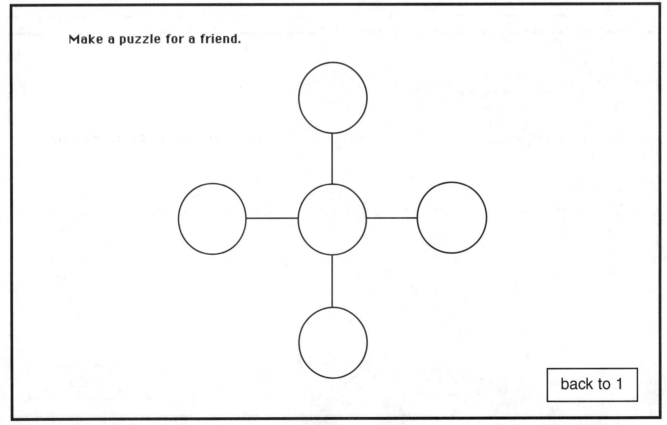

back to 1

FOOD FOR FRIENDS

Divide up plates of food so that each person has an equal amount.

Grade Level: 1–2

Duration: 20 minutes at the computer.

Materials: Computer with multimedia authoring software; printer; multimedia slideshow storyboard on pages 62–63

Before the computer:

- The teacher should create and save the slideshow storyboard on pages 62–63.

- Students should be familiar with using the slideshow feature of multimedia programs. Students should know how to move from slide to slide and how to drag and drop objects on the screen.

- Students should also know how to print slides.

At the computer:

- Display the slideshow file on the monitor.

- Explain to students that they will divide the strawberries so that each person has the same number of strawberries on his or her plate.

- Have students predict how many strawberries each child will get. Ask a student to move 2 of the strawberries and give one to Jon and one to Alexis. Have students continue moving the strawberries in this manner until there are no more on the plate.

- Have students solve the remainder of the problems individually on the computer.

- Ask students to print out their solutions.

- Display the stories along with the solutions on a bulletin board.

- Challenge students to create new problems.

- Remind students to close the file without saving the changes so that others may complete the activity.

Extensions:

- Students can make more problems using different foods and different numbers of plates.

FOOD FOR FRIENDS *(cont.)*

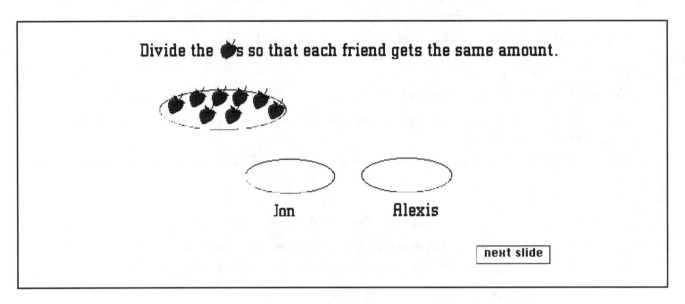

Divide the 🍓s so that each friend gets the same amount.

Jon   Alexis

next slide

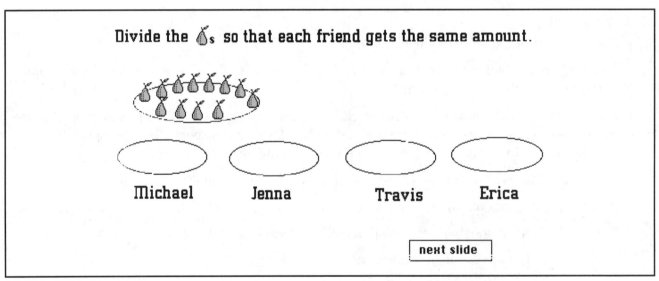

Divide the 🍐s so that each friend gets the same amount.

Michael   Jenna   Travis   Erica

next slide

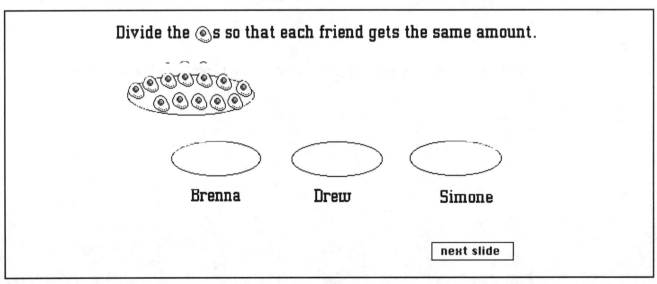

Divide the ◉s so that each friend gets the same amount.

Brenna   Drew   Simone

next slide

FOOD FOR FRIENDS *(cont.)*

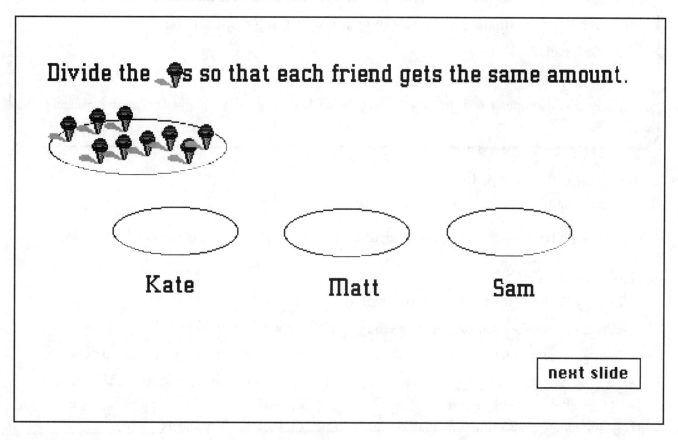

Divide the ⚬s so that each friend gets the same amount.

Kate   Matt   Sam

next slide

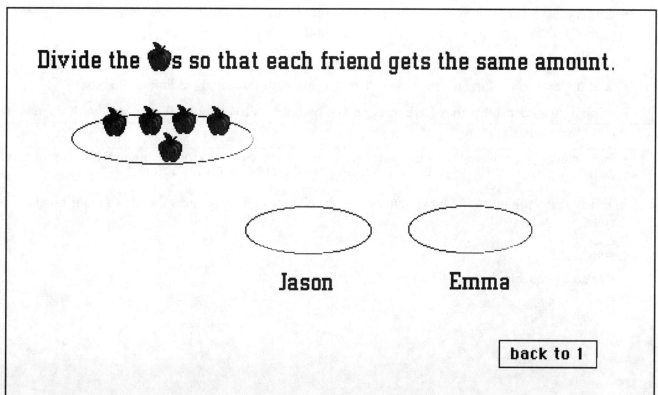

Divide the 🍎s so that each friend gets the same amount.

Jason   Emma

back to 1

COUNTING BY THREES

> **Get ready for multiplication by grouping numbers using paint software.**
>
> **Grade Level:** 2–3
>
> **Duration:** 20–30 minutes at the computer
>
> **Materials:** Computer with paint software; paint file on page 65; copies of the activity sheet on page 66

Before using the computer:

The teacher should create the paint file shown on page 65.

Students should be familiar with the mechanics of dragging and dropping objects in the document.

At the computer:

- Display the paint file in the paint program on the monitor.
- Explain to students that they will be grouping objects in the paint file.
- Point out the first row of objects at the top of the screen. Ask students how many they see.
- Tell students that you want to create groups with three dots in a group. Show students how to draw a circle around a group of three dots.
- Ask students to record the number of dots grouped on their activity sheets.
- Group three more dots by drawing a circle around them. Ask students how many dots have been grouped. Students should record the number on their activity sheet.
- Continue this process until all dots have been grouped.
- Ask students to read the numbers recorded, starting with three and reading until sixty.
- Explain to students that they have just counted by threes. To count by threes, start with three and add three more each time.
- Have students complete this activity on their own for more practice on grouping the dots into sets of three.
- Tell students to close the file without saving the changes. This restores the file to its original state.

Extensions:

- Create a paint file that can be grouped by twos, fives, or tens.

COUNTING BY THREES *(cont.)*

COUNTING BY THREES *(cont.)*

Name _____

1. Write the number of dots in the first group. _____

2. Add the number of dots in the second group to the first group (total number of dots in groups). _____

Continue adding the dots as you group them in threes and record the numbers below.

3. _____

4. _____

5. _____

6. _____

7. _____

8. _____

9. _____

10. _____

11. _____

12. _____

13. _____

14. _____

15. _____

16. _____

17. _____

18. _____

19. _____

20. _____

PATTERN PICTURES

Put the missing pieces in a pattern.

Grade Level: K–1

Duration: 15 minutes at the computer

Materials: Computer with paint software; printer; paint file on page 68

Before the computer:

- The teacher should create a paint file similar to the one on page 68 using whatever stamps he or she thinks will most interest the students.

- Students should be familiar with the stamp function and the delete tools.

- Students should know how to print their drawings.

- Students should be familiar with the concept of patterns.

At the computer:

- Display the print file on the monitor.

- Explain to students that there are patterns that are started on this page but that parts of each pattern are missing. Tell them that their job is to fill in the missing pattern pieces using the stamps from the software program.

- Have students complete the activities on the screen, including making patterns of their own.

- Students should print and turn in their work.

- Post original patterns on a bulletin board for others to solve.

Extensions:

- Students can create and exchange more puzzles.

PATTERN PICTURES *(cont.)*

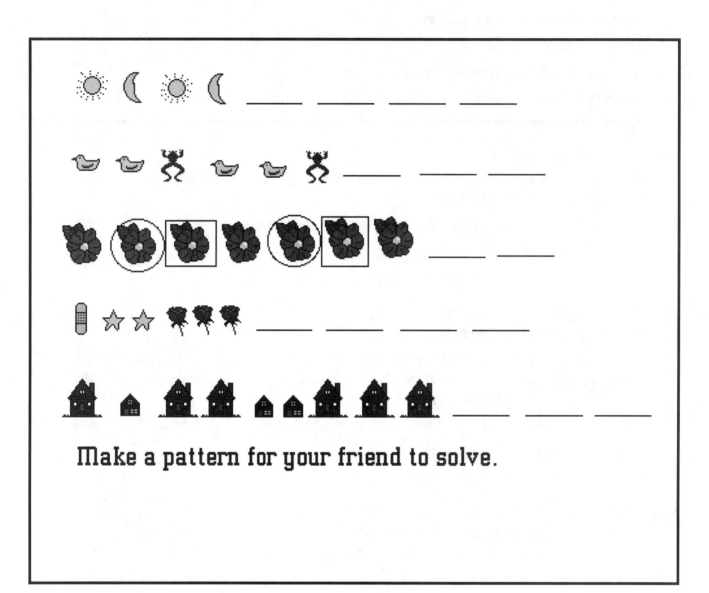

Make a pattern for your friend to solve.

ANDI'S MATCH

> **Practice making different combinations using objects with different attributes.**
>
> **Grade Level:** 1–2
>
> **Duration:** 15–20 minutes at the computer
>
> **Materials:** Computer with paint software; paint file on page 70; copies of activity sheet

Before the computer:

- The teacher should create the paint file shown on page 70. The teacher should also make copies of the activity sheet for each student.

- Students should be familiar with dragging and dropping objects on the screen.

At the computer:

- Display the paint file of Andi's closet on the monitor.

- Explain to students that you are going to tell them a story and they will have to solve the problem.

- Read the following story to the students:

  Andi is getting ready to go see a movie and is deciding what to wear. Andi looks in the closet (point out the closet on the screen). Andi discovers a pair of red pants, a pair of green pants, a pair of blue pants and a pair of yellow pants. Andi also finds a red shirt, a green shirt, a blue shirt and a yellow shirt in the closet. How many different combinations of pants and shirts can Andi choose?

- Remind students that they can drag the clothing items around on the screen to find the answer to the question.

- Have a student create a pants/shirt combination.

- Record the match on the chalkboard or overhead.

- Have another student create a different combination. Record the combination.

- Tell students that they will help Andi find other combinations when they are working on the computer.

- Remind students to record their combinations on the activity sheet as they make them.

- Tell students to close the file and not save the changes. This will restore the file to its original state.

Extensions:

- Students can work in pairs to find the answers to the activity sheet.

- Students can create new stories similar to Andi's that can be developed into paint files for the class.

ANDI'S MATCH *(cont.)*

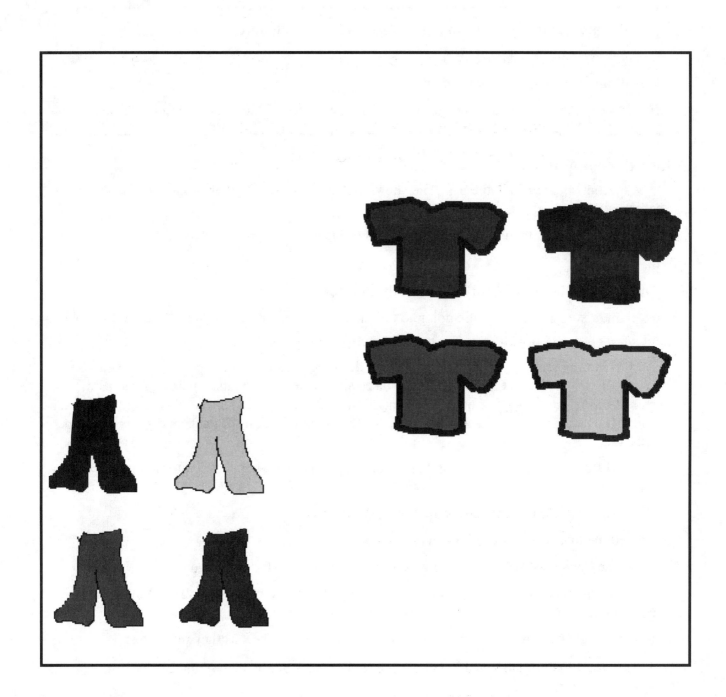

ANDI'S MATCH *(cont.)*

Name _____

Directions: Use the various clothing items in the paint file to find the answers to these questions.

1. How many pairs of pants does Andi have in the closet? _____

2. How many shirts does Andi have in the closet? _____

3. How many matches can you make with the red pants and various shirts? _____

List the matches below:

4. How many matches can you make with the blue pants and various shirts? _____

List the matches below:

5. How many matches can you make with the green pants and various shirts? _____

List the matches below:

6. How many matches can you make with the yellow pants and various shirts? _____

List the matches below:

SHAPELY NUMBERS

Put groups of objects together to form triangles and squares. Look for the patterns in the number of objects.

Grade Level: 1–3

Duration: 15–20 minutes at the computer

Materials: Computer with multimedia authoring software; printer; slideshow storyboard on page 73; student activity page.

Before using the computer:

- The teacher should create and save the slideshow storyboard. Note: You can adjust the pictures on the slideshow to use stamps or holiday clip art instead of circles.

- Students should be familiar with moving through the slides in the slideshow. Students should also know how to drag and drop objects on the screen, how to use the stamp function, and how to print slides.

At the computer:

- Display the first slide on the monitor.

- Explain to students that what they are going to do is to create triangular numbers. Look at the first two groups of objects and discuss what makes 3 and 6 triangular numbers.

- Tell students that they will be making 4 more triangular objects on the screen and printing them out. They will also be recording their findings on the activity sheets.

- Ask students to complete the slideshow and activity sheet by making square numbers.

- Have students print out their solutions and post these on a bulletin board.

Extensions:

- Students can see if it is possible to make other shapes from objects and check if there is any type of pattern that emerges.

SHAPELY NUMBERS *(cont.)*

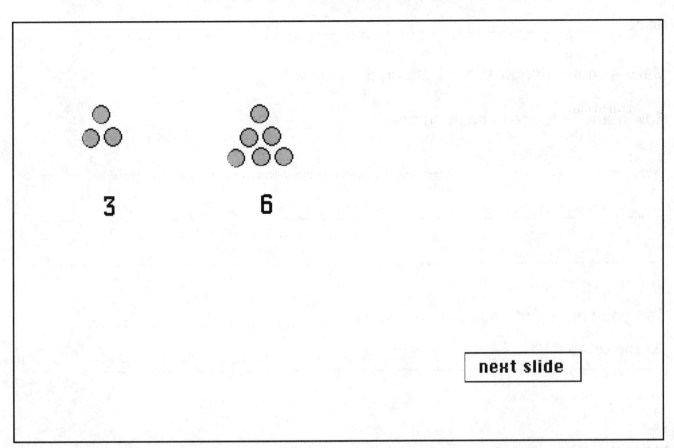

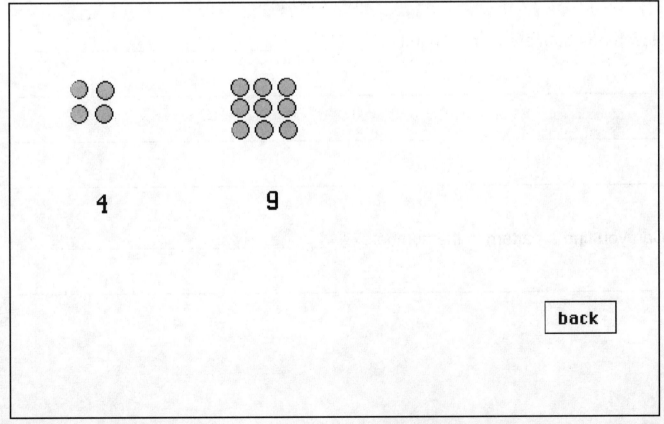

SHAPELY NUMBERS *(cont.)*

Name _____

Make 4 more triangular numbers on the computer.

How many dots are in each number?_____

_____

_____

_____

Can you find a pattern in the numbers? _____

_____

Make 4 more square numbers on the computer.

How many dots are in each number?_____

_____

_____

_____

Can you find a pattern in the numbers? _____

_____

PLODUNKS AND MORE

Figure out what makes a plodunk a plodunk and then create more.

Grade Level: 2–3

Duration: 25 minutes at the computer.

Materials: Computer with multimedia authoring software; printer; multimedia slideshow storyboard on pages 76–78; activity sheet on page 79

Before using the computer:

- The teacher should create and save the slideshow storyboard on pages 76–78.

- The teacher should make a copy of the activity sheet for each student.

- Students should be familiar with using the slideshow feature of multimedia programs. Students should know how to move from slide to slide, how to use the paint and draw tools, and how to drag and drop objects on the screen.

- Students should also know how to print slides.

- Students should be familiar with attributes.

At the computer:

- Ask students if they know what a plodunk is. Explain that today they will find out what a plodunk is and make more plodunks.

- Display the slideshow file on the monitor.

- After students have looked at the objects that are plodunks and those that are not, see if they can tell you one characteristic that all the plodunks have in common.

- When several characteristics have been listed, ask a student to create a plodunk.

- Have students work independently through the multimedia slideshow and solve the remainder of the problems.

- Ask students to print out their solutions.

- Make a bulletin board display with plodunks, sneemers, wilks, droofers and ixes. Post student print outs on the board.

- Remind students to close the file without saving the changes so that others may complete the activity.

Extensions:

- Challenge students to create new groups of creatures with specific characteristics.

PLODUNKS AND MORE *(cont.)*

These are plodunks:

These are not plodunks:

Make some plodunks.

next slide

These are sneemers:

These are not sneemers:

Draw more sneemers.

next slide

PLODUNKS AND MORE *(cont.)*

These are wilks:

These are not wilks:

Draw more wilks.

next slide

These are droofers:

 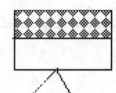 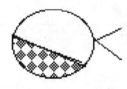

These are not droofers:

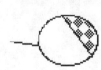 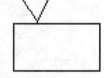

Draw more droofers.

next slide

PLODUNKS AND MORE *(cont.)*

These are ixes:

These are not ixes:

Draw more ixes:

back to page 1

© Teacher Created Materials, Inc.

PLODUNKS AND MORE *(cont.)*

Name _____

What is the rule for plodunks?

Plodunks are _____

_____

_____

What is the rule for sneemers?

Sneemers are _____

_____

_____

What is the rule for wilks?

Wilks are _____

_____

_____

What is the rule for droofers?

Droofers are _____

_____

_____

What is the rule for ixes?

Ixes are _____

_____

_____

WHAT WAS THERE?

> **Practice visual memory skills with disappearing pictures.**
>
> **Grade Level:** 1–2
>
> **Duration:** 25–30 minutes at the computer
>
> **Materials:** Computer with paint software; printer; copies of the activity sheet on page 81

Before the computer:

- The teacher should make a copy of the activity sheet for each student.

- Students should be familiar with the draw tools of the paint program and know how to print their work.

At the computer:

- Begin with a blank document in the paint software.

- Tell students that they are going to make some drawings on the computer using the stamp function and draw tools.

- Explain that after a period of time, they will be asked to remember how these objects looked on the screen and to draw them from memory.

- Direct students to work in pairs at the computer.

- Student B covers his or her eyes while Student A sets up the game.

- Student A draws a large circle and places 5 picture stamps within the circle. The stamps should all be from the category specified on the activity sheet.

- Student A records the names of the picture stamps he or she used on the worksheet while Student B studies the picture on screen.

- Student A selects a new page to cover the original drawing and Student B tries to recreate the original screen from memory using the stamp function.

- Student A can provide hints to help Student B recall any missing object.

- Student B should print out the screen he or she has created.

- Student A reveals the original picture and both students check it with the printed drawing.

Extensions:

- As students demonstrate their proficiency in recalling objects, the number of objects can be increased.

- Students can include objects from several different categories in the same picture to make the game more challenging.

WHAT WAS THERE? *(cont.)*

Name _____

Draw or stamp objects from these categories on the computer screen.

Picture 1—Animals

What pictures did you put in the circle?

1. _____
2. _____
3. _____
4. _____
5. _____

Picture 2—Food

What pictures did you put in the circle?

1. _____
2. _____
3. _____
4. _____
5. _____

Picture 3—Clothing

What pictures did you put in the circle?

1. _____
2. _____
3. _____
4. _____
5. _____

Picture 4—Transportation

What pictures did you put in the circle?

1. _____
2. _____
3. _____
4. _____
5. _____

Picture 5—Toys

What pictures did you put in the circle?

1. _____
2. _____
3. _____
4. _____
5. _____

ANIMAL AND BUG COUNT

> **Create pictures on the computer to help solve number problems.**
>
> **Grade Level:** 1–2
>
> **Duration:** 20–30 minutes on the computer
>
> **Materials:** Computer with paint software; printer; copies of activity sheet on page 83

Before using the computer:

- The teacher should change the objects to be drawn on the activity sheet to correspond with stamps that are available in the class software program.

- The teacher should make a copy of the activity sheet for each student.

- Students should be familiar with paint and draw tools of the software and know how to use the print function.

At the computer:

Begin with a blank document in the paint software.

- Tell students that they will use the stamp function or paint and draw tools to draw the animals described on the activity sheet.

- Have a student read the first problem on the activity sheet.

- Ask a student to stamp or draw three ladybugs beside eachother on the screen.

- Ask students how many legs a ladybug has. Ask students if all the ladybug's legs are visible on the screen. If they are not, have a student draw them in.

- Ask students how they might find out how many legs three ladybugs have.

- Have students count the legs on the three ladybugs and write their answer on the activity sheet.

- Let students continue through the problems on the activity sheet, working independently at the computer.

- Remind students to write their answers on the activity sheet.

- Have students print their screens of stamped or drawn objects to turn in with the activity sheet.

- After students have completed the activity sheet, ask them to explain how answers were reached using the pictures.

Extensions:

- Students can create seasonal or theme related problems to solve.

- Students can create problems for other students to solve.

ANIMAL AND BUG COUNT *(cont.)*

Name _____

1. Draw 3 ladybugs.

   How many legs are there when 3 ladybugs walk on the window sill? _____

2. Draw 4 bluebirds.

   How many wings are there on 4 bluebirds? _____

3. Draw 6 puppies.

   How many ears are there on 6 puppies?_____

4. Draw 5 frogs.

   How many legs do 5 frogs have? _____

5. Draw 7 cats.

   How many tails can wag when 7 cats are in the room? _____

CANDY STORE CRAZE

Find the solution to these word problems by drawing the problems.

Grade Level: 1–2

Duration: 15–20 minutes at the computer

Materials: Computer with paint program; printer; copies of activity sheet on page 85

Before using the computer:

- The teacher should have copies of the activity sheet on page 85 available to each student.
- Students should be familiar with the draw and paint tools in the software program. Students should also know how to print.

At the computer:

- Display a blank document in the paint program on the monitor.
- Tell students they are going to solve some word problems using the computer to draw the pictures.
- Have a student read the first problem on the activity sheet.
- Ask a student to draw the candy pieces described in the problem. Students may use the stamp feature or any of the paint tools available to draw a simplified picture of the candy pieces. Help the student if necessary.
- Have students solve the problem using the pictures as needed.
- Ask students to solve the remainder of the problems on their own.
- Have students print their drawings to turn in with the completed activity sheet.

Extensions:

- Students can create seasonal and theme related problems.

CANDY STORE CRAZE *(cont.)*

Name _____

The candy store has been quite busy. Solve the problems below using the computer to draw the pictures.

1. Paul's mother bought him 3 candy canes at the store. Paul bought 2 grape lollipops too. Later his uncle gave him 5 jawbreakers. He put all the candy in a bag. How many pieces of candy does Paul have? Draw the candy that is in Paul's bag.

2. Linda got 5 chocolate drops from her Aunt Lisa. Tommy gave Linda his coconut ball and Jose gave her his 4 lemon cubes. Linda bought 2 peppermint patties from the candy store. How many pieces of candy does Linda have? Draw the candy.

3. Carlita gave Paul 4 lemon drops, Charlie 6 cinnamon drops, and Marcie 7 red hot candies. How many candies did she give away? Draw them all.

4. Tabitha decided to split her candy with Maria. She gave Maria 2 malted milk balls, 5 jelly beans, and 4 jawbreakers. If she split her candy evenly, how much candy did she have to start with? Draw your answer.

5. The candy store owner gave Larry and David a bag of candy. Each boy had 2 chocolate bars, 5 gummy worms, 3 caramels and 2 licorice sticks. How many pieces of candy did the store owner give away? Draw your answer.

PAINTING WORD PROBLEMS

> **Draw solutions to story problems using paint software.**
>
> **Grade Level:** 1–3
>
> **Duration:** 20–30 minutes at the computer
>
> **Materials:** Computer with paint software; printer; copies of activity sheet on page 87

Before the computer:

- The teacher should make available copies of the activity sheet for each student.

- Students should be familiar with solving word problems with manipulatives. Students should also be familiar with the draw and paint tools and the stamp function of the software.

At the computer:

- Display a blank paint document.

- Explain to students that they are going to use the paint program to draw solutions to word problems.

- Have a student read the first problem.

- Ask students for ideas on how to draw this problem. Any solution that includes drawing the pieces of candy and adding up their cost will work.

- If stamps are available, allow students to use them to "draw out" the solution.

- Have students record the answers on their activity sheets.

- Remind students that if a particular solution does not work, they can easily erase that solution and try another one on the computer. Show students how to delete drawings.

- Allow students to work through the remainder of the problems individually. Remind them to record their answers on the activity sheet.

- Have students print out their drawings to turn in with the activity sheet.

Extensions:

- Students can create new word problems to solve.

PAINTING WORD PROBLEMS *(cont.)*

Name _____

1. Mia had 23¢ to spend at the candy store. She wanted to buy at least 4 pieces of candy. The signs in the window read:

   Lollipop . . . . 5¢
   Peppermint . . . . 6¢
   Chocolate bar . . . . 10¢
   Gummy worm . . . . 2¢
   Lemon drops . . . . 1¢
   Jawbreakers . . . . 3¢

What are the different combinations of candy Mia can buy? Draw your answers.

2. Joey went to the library. He knew he could check out 4 books or 8 magazines or a combination of the two. What are the possible combinations of books and magazines Joey can check out? Draw your answers. (Hint: How many magazines can be checked out for each book?)

3. Paul and Myra went to the fruit stand with 35¢. They wanted to buy fruit for themselves and three of their friends. They found out that:

   A pear costs 5¢.   A peach costs 3¢.
   An apple costs 8¢.   An orange costs 9¢.
   A plum costs 7¢.

What can Paul and Myra buy so that each person has a piece of fruit and they do not have any money left over?

What fruit can they buy for themselves and their friends and still have money left over?

Draw your answers.

4. Josh, Martin and Tyrone are trading baseball cards. Tyrone has a special card that he said he would trade for 3 of Martin's hologram cards or 5 of Josh's regular cards. Josh saw that Tyrone had 2 more of these special cards. How many cards does Josh need to trade for all of Tyrone's special cards? How many does Martin need to trade for all of Tyrone's special cards?

PAINTING WORD PROBLEMS *(cont.)*

Draw your answers. If Tyrone traded all of his special cards, what could he get in return? Draw the possible combinations.

5. Sarah went to the flower shop to buy flowers for her mother.   She had 95¢.
   She wanted to buy at least six flowers to make a bouquet. Sarah knew that:

   A daisy costs 12¢.   A lily costs 15¢.
   A carnation costs 5¢.   A rose costs17¢.
   An iris costs 12¢.   A baby's breath costs 13¢ a bunch.

   What flowers can Sarah buy to make a bouquet and spend all of her money? What flowers can she buy to make a bouquet and have money left over? Draw your answers.

SNOWMAN DANCE

Practice logical thinking and problem solving with these visual puzzles.

Grade Level: 2–3

Duration: 20–25 minutes at the computer.

Materials: Computer with multimedia authoring software; printer; multimedia slideshow storyboard on pages 91–93

Before the computer:

- The teacher should create and save the slideshow storyboard on pages 91–93.

- Students should be familiar with using the slideshow feature of multimedia programs. They should know how to move from slide to slide and how to drag and drop objects on the screen. Students should also know how to print slides.

At the computer:

- Display the slideshow file of snowmen on the monitor.

- Explain to students that they will place the snowmen in the correct order to solve the story problems on the activity sheet.

- Have a student read the first problem.

- Ask students to tell you which snowman should go first, second, and so forth until the snowmen are in the correct order.

- If someone gives an incorrect answer, read that part of the story problem again.

- When the first slide is completed, ask students to share their problem solving approach.

- Have students solve the remainder of the problems individually on the computer.

- Ask students to print out their solutions.

- Display the stories along with the solutions on a bulletin board.

- Challenge students to create new problems.

- Remind students to close the file without saving the changes so that others may complete the activity.

Extensions:

- Students can solve problems involving animals, spring flowers, or anything else that interests them.

- More snowmen can be added to increase the possibilities and complexity of problems.

- Addition and subtraction problems can be worked out with the snowmen appearing or disappearing from slides.

WORD PROBLEMS FOR SNOWMAN DANCE

Name _____

Problem 1

Five snowmen were lined up on a hill. Two were wearing red hats, one had a blue hat, one had a green hat, and one had an orange hat. The one with the blue hat was between the two with the red hats. The green hat was behind both of the red hats. The orange hat was behind the green hat. How did the snowmen line up?

Problem 2

Five snowmen were lined up on a hill. One was wearing a yellow scarf. Two were wearing blue scarves. Two were wearing brown scarves. The one with the yellow scarf was behind the two with the blue scarves. The two with the brown scarves were in front of the two with the blue scarves. How did the snowmen line up? Who was last in line?

Problem 3

Five snowmen were lined up in the front yard. Two snowmen had one button. Two snowmen had three buttons and one snowman had two buttons. The one with two buttons was in front of the two with one button. The two with three buttons were behind the two with one button. How did they line up? Who was first in line?

Problem 4

Five snowmen danced down the street. One had on yellow mittens. Two had on blue mittens. One had on purple mittens and one had on red mittens. The one with red mittens was behind the two with blue mittens. The one with yellow mittens was in front of the two with blue mittens. The one with purple mittens was behind the one with red mittens. How did they line up? Who was third in line?

Problem 5

Five snowmen stood in the field. Two snowmen had one bird sitting on their heads. One snowman had two birds on his head. One snowman had three birds on his head. One snowman had four birds on his head. The one with four birds was in front of the one with two birds. The one with three birds was behind the two with one bird. The two with one bird were in front of the one with four birds. How did they line up? Who was second in line? Who was last in line?

STORYBOARD FOR SNOWMAN DANCE

Notes on Construction of the Slides:

Use multimedia slide presentation software. The snowmen can be made from clip art or drawn using the circle tool. Add hats, mittens, scarves, buttons, and birds with stamps or by drawing. Be sure that the snowmen are draggable. If you run into a problem making the snowmen draggable, check the software manual.

Each button at the bottom of the slide should take the student to the next slide. The button on the last slide can signal the end or take the student back to the first slide.

Be sure the slides contain the following items:

Slide one:

5 snowmen—two with red hats, one with a blue hat, one with a green hat and one with an orange hat.

Slide two:

5 snowmen—one with a yellow scarf, two with blue scarves, two with brown scarves.

Slide three:

5 snowmen—two with one button, two with three buttons, one with two buttons.

Slide four:

5 snowmen—one with yellow mittens, two with blue mittens, one with purple mittens, one with red mittens.

Slide five:

5 snowmen—two with one bird on the head, one with two birds on the head, one with three birds on the head and one with four birds on the head.

next slide

STORYBOARD FOR SNOWMAN DANCE *(cont.)*

next slide

next slide

STORYBOARD FOR SNOWMAN DANCE *(cont.)*

THE COSTUME LINE-UP

> **Solve these word puzzles by manipulating characters and using logical thinking skills.**
>
> **Grade Level:** 2–3
>
> **Duration:** 15–20 minutes at the computer
>
> **Materials:** Computer with multimedia authoring software; printer; slideshow storyboard on pages 95 and 96; student activity page

Before the computer:

- The teacher should create and save the slideshow storyboard. Note: It may be necessary to adjust the pictures on the slideshow and activity sheet depending on what stamps or clip art is available in your software program.
- Students should be familiar with how to move through the slides in the slideshow. Students should also know how to drag and drop objects on the screen and how to print slides.

At the computer:

- Display the first slide on the monitor.
- Explain to students that they are going to solve word problems on the computer.
- Read the first problem to the students.
- Ask students which figure they think should be first.
- Demonstrate to students how to move that figure to the correct place on the slide.
- Ask which figure should come next and have a student drag that figure into place.
- Continue this until all the figures are in their correct places.
- Have students explain how they solved the problem.
- Ask students to solve the remaining problems on the computer individually.
- Have students print out their solutions and post these on a bulletin board.

Extensions:

- More figures can be added to the slides to make the line-up longer.
- Other themes can be used for the slides.
- Students can write the ordinal numbers under the figures on their activity sheets.
- Students can work in groups to create new problems.

COSTUME LINE-UP STORYBOARD

Slide 3

Slide 2

Slide 1

Notes on Construction of the Slides:

Use multimedia slide presentation software. The figures should be made from stamps or other clip art. Be sure that the figures are draggable. If you run into a problem making them draggable, check the software manual.

Each button at the bottom of the slide should take the student to the next slide. The button on the last slide can signal the end or take the student back to the first slide.

Slides one through five should contain any 5 costume-type figures that are available to you. Adjust worksheet and slides accordingly.

Ghost = _____

Monster = _____

Witch = _____

Jack-O-Lantern = _____

Scarecrow = _____

COSTUME LINE-UP STORYBOARD *(cont.)*

Slide 5

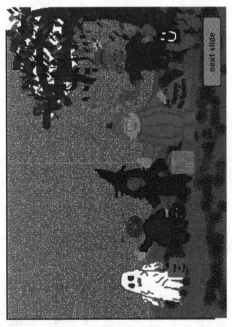

Slide 4

THE COSTUME LINE-UP

Name _____

Read the problem. Move the figures around on the slide to determine the correct order. Print the slideshow and turn it in with this activity sheet.

1. Five children were going to a costume party: a ghost, a monster, a witch, a jack-o-lantern, and a scarecrow. The ghost was first in line. The monster was second and the jack-o-lantern was next. The witch was last with the scarecrow in front of her. Put the children in the correct order. Who is fourth in line?

2. Five children were going to a costume party: a ghost, a monster, a witch, a jack-o-lantern, and a scarecrow. The monster was last. The witch stood in front of the monster. The jack-o-lantern was first and the ghost came next. The scarecrow was in the middle. Put the children in the correct order. Who was third in line?

3. Five children were going to a costume party: a ghost, a monster, a witch, a jack-o-lantern, and a scarecrow. The ghost came before the witch. The witch came before the jack-o-lantern. The scarecrow came behind the jack-o-lantern. The monster came last. Put the children in the correct order. Who was fourth in line?

4. Five children were going to a costume party: a ghost, a monster, a witch, a jack-o-lantern, and a scarecrow. The monster was behind the ghost. The ghost was behind the witch. The witch was behind the jack-o-lantern. The jack-o-lantern was behind the scarecrow. Put the children in the correct order. Who is second in line?

5. Five children were going to a costume party: a ghost, a monster, a witch, a jack-o-lantern, and a scarecrow. The scarecrow was behind the monster and in front of the ghost. The witch was in front of the monster. The jack-o-lantern was behind the ghost. Put the children in the correct order. Who was fifth in line?

THE COSTUME LINE-UP *(cont.)*

Challenge problems:

6. Five children were going to a costume party: a ghost, a monster, a witch, a jack-o-lantern, and a scarecrow. If the scarecrow was behind the monster, who was behind the witch, who was in front of the jack-o-lantern, who was in front of the ghost, who was first in line?

7. Five children were going to a costume party: a ghost, a monster, a witch, a jack-o-lantern, and a scarecrow. If the scarecrow was first in line, the monster was last, the ghost was behind the scarecrow, and the witch was in front of the monster, where was the jack-o-lantern?

8. Five children were going to a costume party: a ghost, a monster, a witch, a jack-o-lantern, and a scarecrow. If the monster was last and the witch was in front of him with the scarecrow in front of her and the jack-o-lantern in front of him, who was first in line?

RIDDLES TO PAINT

> **Create pictures on the computer to help visualize solutions to story problems.**
>
> **Grade Level:** 2–3
>
> **Duration:** 20–30 minutes at the computer
>
> **Materials:** Computer with paint software; printer; copies of the activity sheet on page 100

Before the computer:

- The teacher should make a copy of the activity sheet for each student.

- Students should be familiar with the stamp function and the draw and paint tools. Students should also know how to print their drawings.

At the computer:

- Display a blank document in the paint software on the monitor.

- Explain to students that there are story problems on the activity sheet to solve and that they may draw the problems out with stamps or with the paint and draw tools.

- Place a number one at the top of the document.

- Ask a student to read question number one.

- Use the stamps of people or draw simple stick figures to illustrate the story.

- Ask students to determine what the answer is and to record the answer on their activity sheet.

- Have students complete the activity sheet on an individual basis. They should use the paint program to draw the story problems.

- Students should print their pictures to turn in along with the activity sheet.

Extensions:

- Students can create new puzzles for other students to solve.

RIDDLES TO PAINT *(cont.)*

Name _____

1. Jeff is making sandwiches for his friends. Scott and Miguel are there, and so are Pablo and Jenny. Sandra and Mark are knocking at the door.

   How many sandwiches should Jeff make if he is hungry too? _____

2. Paula is trying to guess how many pieces of candy her teacher has in the box. Her teacher tells her that it is more than 12 and is an odd number. The number of pieces of candy can be grouped into three groups, with no pieces left over.

   How many pieces of candy are in the box? _____

3. Lora wants to buy pizza for a party. She knows 10 friends are coming. She thinks each friend will eat 1 piece each.   The pizza man tells her that each pizza has 4 pieces in it.

   How many pizzas should Lora buy? _____

4. David is collecting leaves. He has a leaf with 3 points and another with 1 point. He has 2 leaves with 4 points and another with 5 points.

   How many points are on all the leaves together? _____

5. Jon and Matt each walk across a lawn covered with snow. Jon's dog comes too and his cat follows behind. Draw the footprints the boys and the animals leave behind.

   How many footprints did the boys leave?_____ the dog?_____ the cat?_____

COLORS AND SHAPES

Follow directions to create geometric shapes of different colors.

Grade Level: K–1

Duration: 20–30 minutes at the computer

Materials: Computer with paint software; printer; models of basic geometric shapes

Before the computer:

- The teacher should review basic geometric shapes with students using models from a math kit or made from posterboard.

- The teacher should make a copy of the activity sheet for each student.

- Practice identifying these words: draw, big, little. Be sure the students can recognize color words.

- Students should be familiar with using the paint and draw tools and should know how to print.

- Students should also know how to use the floodfill tool (paint bucket icon on most paint software programs).

At the computer:

- Display a blank screen on the monitor.

- Explain to students that they are going to follow directions and create shapes of different sizes and colors.

- Have a student use the paint tool to draw a circle. Ask another student to color it brown.

- Give each student the activity sheet and have them work on it at the computer independently. If they are unable to identify color words or the words big, little, and draw, you may wish to have an older student assist them.

- Have students print their work to turn in with the activity sheet.

Extensions:

- Students can make problems like these for friends to solve.

- Students can put these shapes together to create a picture.

COLORS AND SHAPES *(cont.)*

Name _____

1. Draw a little ◯ .
   Color it green.

2. Draw a big ☐ .
   Color it purple.

3. Draw a ☐ .
   Color it yellow.

4. Draw a big ◯ .
   Color it blue.

5. Draw a little ☐ .
   Color it red.

FUN WITH FACES

Create entertaining faces using geometric shapes.

Grade Level: K–1

Duration: 10–15 minutes at the computer

Materials: Computer with multmedia authoring software; slideshow storyboard on pages 104–107

Before the computer:

- The teacher should use the paint tools in the multimedia software to draw the faces on pages 104–106. Blank slides should be between the face slides. All slides should have a button that moves to the next slide.

- Students should be familiar with the basic shapes of circle, rectangle, square, and triangle, and should know how to use paint tools to draw them.

- Students should know how to print slides.

At the computer:

- Explain to students that they are going to see faces appear on the computer screen. The faces will come up one at a time and then disappear.

- Tell students to look closely for different shapes in the faces.

- Display the first slide on the monitor.

- Have students point out the different shapes they see in the faces.

- Move to the second screen which is blank. Ask a student to use the circle tool and draw the face.

- Have other students add the eyes, nose, and mouth with other shape tools. Move back to the first slide to check for accuracy.

- Have students click on the slide button to move to the next face and work independently to draw the face on the blank slide. Repeat until all five faces have been created.

- Have students print out the slideshow when finished with their own drawings.

- Remind students not to save their changes so that others can use the original file.

Extensions:

- Students can create their own faces to add to the slide show.

- Students can type a sentence about each face using the text tool.

STORYBOARD FOR FUN WITH FACES

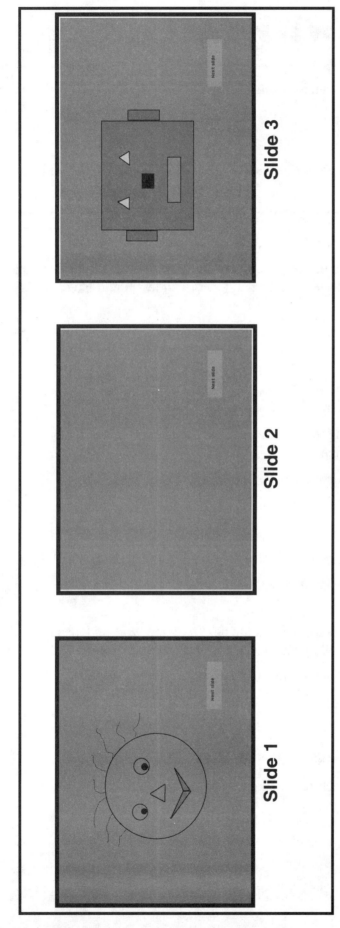

Slide 1

Slide 2

Slide 3

Notes on slideshow:

Use the draw tools to create the faces in the slideshow.

Be sure that there is a button at the bottom of each slide to take the students to the next slide. The button on the last slide can signal the end or take the students back to the first slide.

If you wish, you can put a timer on the face slides and set the amount of time that you want the students to see the face before moving to the next slide. Do not set a timer on the blank slides so that students have enough time to draw.

You may also wish to put a button on the blank slide so that students can go back and look at the face again.

STORYBOARD FOR FUN WITH FACES *(cont.)*

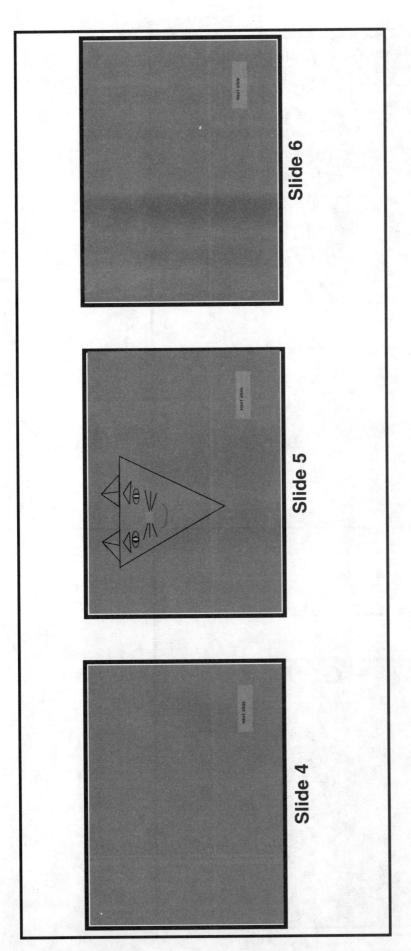

Slide 4

Slide 5

Slide 6

STORYBOARD FOR FUN WITH FACES *(cont.)*

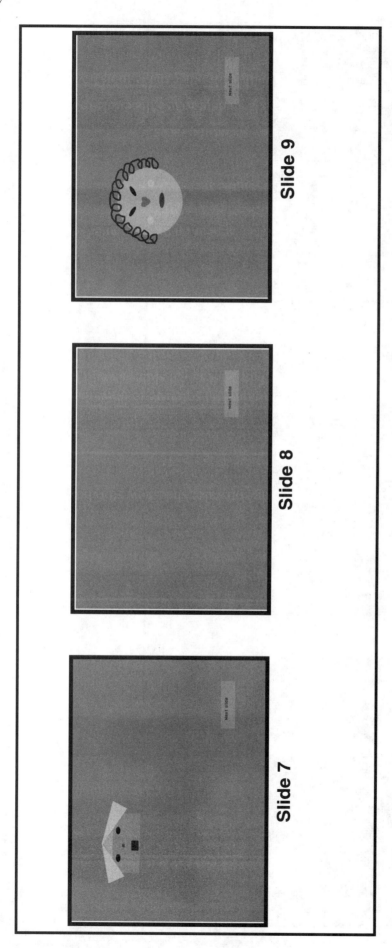

Slide 7

Slide 8

Slide 9

STORYBOARD FOR FUN WITH FACES *(cont.)*

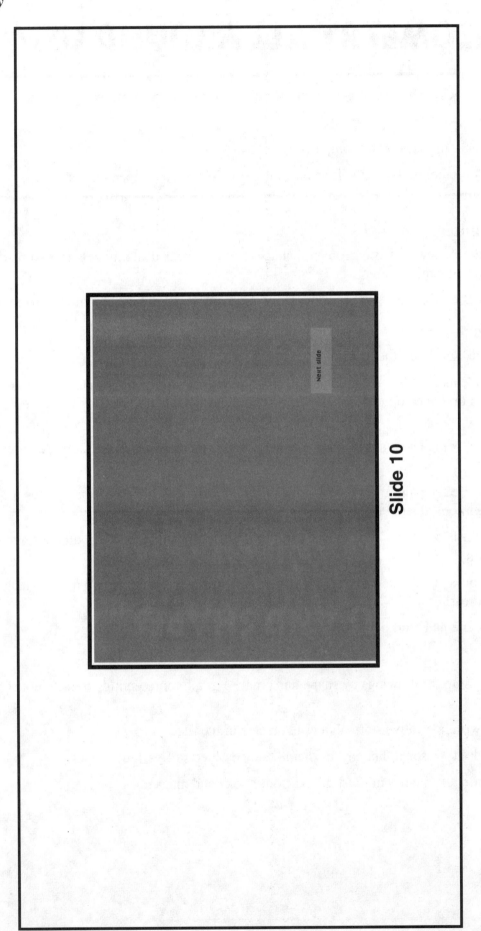

Slide 10

GEOMETRY ALL AROUND US

Help students become aware of geometric shapes in their surroundings.

Grade Level: K–1

Duration: 20–30 minutes at the computer

Materials: Computer with paint software; printer; models of basic geometric shapes

Before the computer:

- The teacher should review basic geometric shapes with students using models from a math kit or made from posterboard.
- Students should be familiar with using the paint and draw tools and should know how to print.

At the computer:

- Display a blank screen on the monitor.
- Explain to students that they are going to look for geometric shapes in objects around the room and draw them on the computer screen. If in a computer lab, have students imagine items in their own classroom.
- Point out some examples of shapes such as the rectangle on the teacher's desk or the circle on the clock.
- Have students use the paint tools to draw one of the objects with the geometric shapes mentioned and use the text tool to label the shape.
- Ask students for examples of other shapes and have them draw those objects on the screen and label them with the text tool.
- Repeat this process until students have identified and drawn objects using all of the shapes that were reviewed earlier.
- Print the class file and bind into a shape book.

Extensions:

- Students can group the drawings by shape and create a graph representing the different shapes drawn.
- Students can write a creative story about the objects in the file.
- Students can draw seasonal, holiday, or theme related objects of various shapes.
- Students can identify shapes in illustrations from books and magazines.

SHAPE PAINTINGS

Use paint software to create original drawings and reinforce knowledge of shapes.

Grade Level: K–2

Duration: 15–20 minutes at the computer

Materials: Computer with paint software; copies of activity sheet on page 110

Before the computer:

- The teacher should make copies of the activity sheet for each student.

- Students should be familiar with the paint functions of the software and should be able to draw a triangle, rectangle, square and circle on the screen.

At the computer:

- Display a blank document in the paint program on the monitor.

- Tell students that they will be making pictures using specific shapes.

- Show students how to draw simple geometric shapes using the various paint tools. Demonstrate a circle, square, triangle, and rectangle.

- Demonstrate how to use the floodfill tool (paint bucket icon in most paint programs) to fill in the shapes with color.

- Have students follow the directions on the activity sheet to create their shape paintings. Explain that the shapes in the picture can be any size they choose.

- Remind students to print their work. These printed drawings should be attached to the answer sheet.

- Display paintings on bulletin boards for future reference of geometric shapes.

Extensions:

- Students can determine different shapes to be included in new pictures.

SHAPE PAINTINGS

Name _____

Directions: Make pictures on the computer using these shapes. Print out the pictures and attach them to this page.

1. Make a picture with △ △ △ ○ ○ ☐

2. Make a picture with ○ ○ ○ ☐ ☐ ☐ ☐

3. Make a picture with ☐ ☐ ○ ○ ☐ △ △

4. Make a picture with △ ○ ☐ ☐ ☐ ☐

5. Make a picture with as many shapes as you wish.

How many △ ? _____

How many ○ ? _____

How many ☐ ? _____

How many ☐ ? _____

PUZZLING PAINTINGS

Create tesselations and learn more about patterns and geometric figures.

Grade Level: 2–3

Duration: 20 to 30 minutes at the computer over two to three days.

Materials: Computer with paint software; two dimensional geometric shapes; models of tessellated patterns such as tiling or geometric tiles (these can be paper or cardboard tiles) (Note: tessellations are similar to tile patterns.)

Before the computer:

- The teacher should introduce or review two dimensional geometric shapes including octagon, square, rectangle, triangle, and circle. The teacher should also show students examples of tiling either in pictures or on the school site (sometimes the cafeteria or bathroom will have tiled walls with tessellated patterns). The teacher may want students to draw a tessellated pattern on paper before using the computer. This can be done by having students trace geometric tiles or their own tiles made from heavy paper and coloring these tiles to make a patterned puzzle.

- Students should be familiar with paint and draw tools in the software and should know how to use the basic draw tools.

- Students should also be familiar with the copy and paste function.

- Students should know how to print their work.

At the computer:

- Display a blank document in the paint program on the monitor.

- Tell students that they will be making tessellated patterns on the computer.

- Show students how to draw simple geometric shapes using the various paint tools.

- Show students how to copy and paste these shapes into a pattern.

- Tell students that it is important when making the pattern to not have any spaces between the shapes. The shapes should fit into each other exactly.

- Encourage students to use only one or two different shapes in a small area to get a tight fit. Some students may require assistance in creating the tight fit—you may want to help them get the first "fit."

- After students have a tight fit for their pieces, show students how to copy and paste the selected shapes repeatedly to create a puzzle pattern or a chain pattern.

- Demonstrate how to use the floodfill tool (paint bucket icon in most paint programs) to fill in the shapes with color.

PUZZLING PAINTINGS *(cont.)*

At the computer: *(cont.)*

- Have students print their patterns.

- Pair students to exchange puzzles. Have each partner identify the geometric shapes used to create the pattern.

- Display printed patterns on a bulletin board.

Extensions:

- Students can make a chain of two different shapes such as the one on page 113. They can then be guided to make rows of these chains to create a pattern.

- Students can create other patterns with geometric shapes.

- Students can use three shapes to create a pattern.

- Students can look for patterns on the walls, floors, objects, etc.

PUZZLING PAINTINGS *(cont.)*

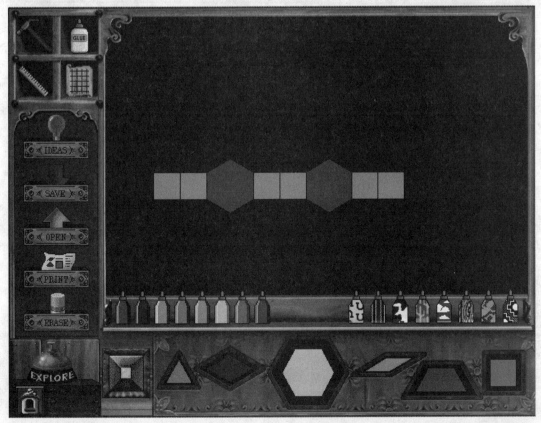

PUZZLING PAINTINGS *(cont.)*

SOFTWARE CONNECTION:

Suggested software: *Carnival Countdown* by Edmark

"Annie's Pattern Block Roundup" module allows students to practice manipulating geometric shapes in the Explore mode.

From the opening screen, go to Annie's Pattern Block Roundup by clicking on the saloon doors. After Annie appears, click on the bell to go to explore mode.

Students can choose from among six different geometric shapes. They can build an infinite number of designs using these shapes and then also have the option to color them.

Students that need help getting started can click on the "Ideas" button and see several different patterns and designs made from combining different shapes. They can try to recreate these designs or invent some new ones of their own.

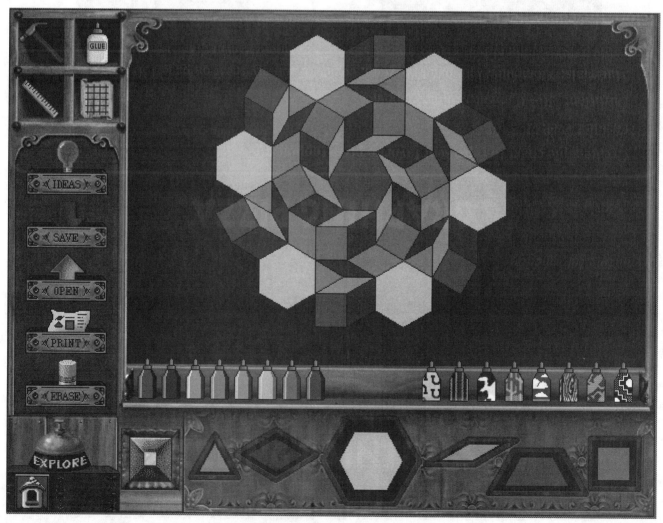

JACK'S FACE

Create and graph various jack-o-lantern faces.

Grade Level: 1–2

Duration: 30 minutes or more at the computer

Materials: Computer with a paint program; printer; file with pumpkin outline as shown on page 117; file with graph template as shown on page 118

Before the computer:

- The teacher should discuss jack-o-lantern faces. Stories about jack-o-lanterns can be read to introduce the lesson.

- The teacher should also review the concept of graphing.

- The teacher should create and save two files—one with a pumpkin outline and one with a graph template.

- Students should be familiar with paint and draw tools in the paint software.

- Students should also be familiar with how to print.

At the computer:

Part I

- Display the pumpkin outline in the file on the monitor.

- Explain to students that they will create a face for the pumpkin to become a jack-o-lantern.

- Show students how to use the paint tools to draw the face.

- Demonstrate to students how to use the floodfill (paint bucket icon in most paint programs) to fill in the eyes, nose, and mouth.

- Have students draw the jack-o-lantern face of their choice without looking at other jack-o-lantern faces that have been drawn.

- Have students print their jack-o-lantern faces and write their names on the back side.

- Remind students to close the file and not save the changes. This restores the file to its original state.

JACK'S FACE *(cont.)*

Part II

- Have all students stand in a circle holding their drawings in front of them for class viewing.

- Tell students that they are going to group the jack-o-lantern faces by appearance and create a graph on the computer.

- Ask students to determine which category their jack-o-lantern fits into:

  Sad faces
  Happy faces
  Silly faces
  Scary/mean looking faces

- Have students whose faces fall into a particular category stand together. When all faces have been placed into groups, ask the class to count the number of jack-o-lanterns in each category. Record the information on an overhead or blackboard.

- Display the graph template in the paint program on the monitor.

- Ask students how many jack-o-lantern faces are happy.

- Have a student draw circles in the happy face box to represent the number of children who drew happy face jack-o-lanterns.

- Ask students how many jack-o-lanterns are in the other categories.

- Have different students draw circles in the correct boxes to represent the number of jack-o-lanterns in each category.

- Lead a class discussion about the graph by asking questions similar to the following:

  How many pumpkins are in the happy faces category?

  How many are in the sad faces category?

  Which is the smallest group?

  Which is the largest group?

- Ask students to use the information gathered to create their own picture graph by selecting the symbol they want to use to represent the number of children who drew particular faces.

- Have students print their graphs and turn them in with their jack-o-lantern faces.

- Remind students to close the file without saving it. This will allow others to use the blank graph.

Extensions:

- Students can graph the jack-o-lantern faces in different ways, such as by round eyes, square eyes, triangle nose, round nose, etc.

- Students can select a jack-o-lantern face for the class jack-o-lantern.

JACK'S FACE *(cont.)*

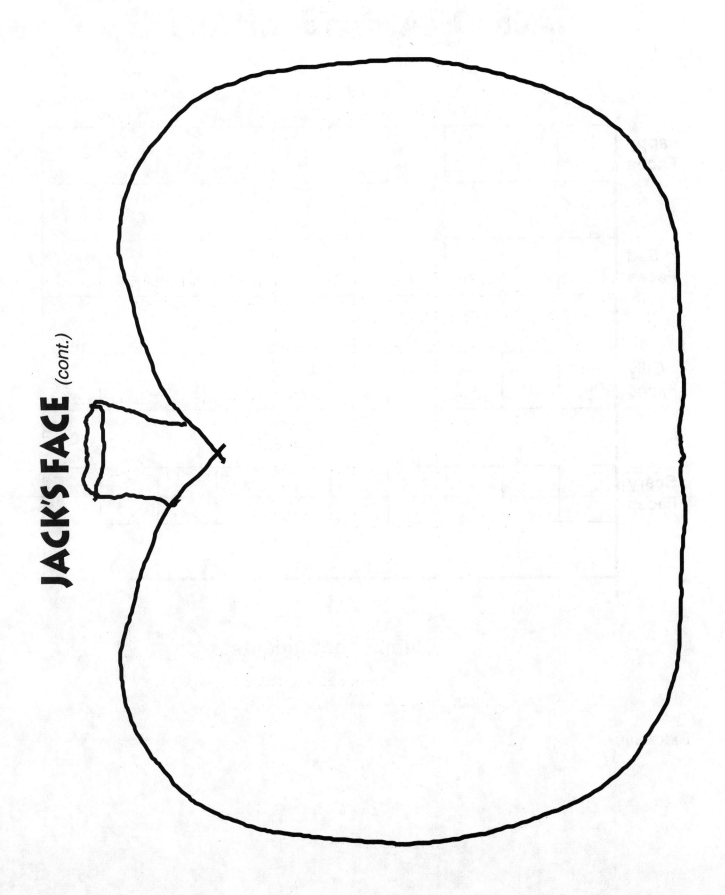

JACK-O-LANTERN CHART

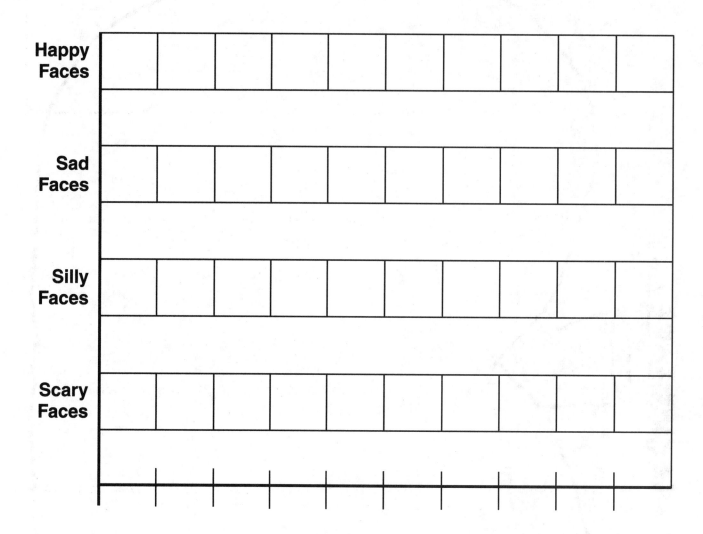

Number of Students

THE COOKIE TASTE TEST

Collect and organize data and then display it on the computer.

Grade Level: 1–2

Duration: 40–45 minutes over two days

Materials: Computer with paint program; printer; different kinds of cookies broken into bite-size pieces; colored paper plates; file of chart template on page 121

Before using the computer:

- The teacher should create the graph template on page 121 and save it in a file.

- The teacher should break the cookies into bite-size pieces and place them on differently colored plates. Each type of cookie should be on a different plate.

- Students should be familiar with the paint and draw tools in the paint program.

- Students should taste the different brands of cookies and decide which brand they like best. They should remember which color plate the cookie was on.

At the computer:

- Lead a class discussion on the tasting by asking students to raise their hands for the plate of cookies they liked best.

- Count the number of raised hands for each color and record these numbers on the overhead or blackboard.

- Tell students that they are going to make a picture graph of their findings using the computer.

- Display the graph template in the paint program on the monitor.

- Explain to students that they are going to use a circle for each person who voted for a particular brand of cookie.

- Ask students how many of them liked the cookies on the red plate.

- Have a student draw the number of circles in the red box to represent the number of children who liked the cookies on the red plate best.

- Ask about the remaining plates of cookies and have students fill in the graph with the appropriate number of circles.

- Lead a class discussion about the graph by asking questions similar to the following:

    Which cookie was preferred by most of the students?

    Which cookie was liked the least?

    How many students liked the second favorite cookie?

    Is there a kind of cookie that no one liked?

    Can you think of any other ways to show the same information about the cookies?

THE COOKIE TASTE TEST *(cont.)*

At the computer: *(cont.)*

- Tell students that they will have the opportunity to create their own picture graph by selecting the symbol they want to use to represent the number of children who liked a particular cookie.

- Tell students to print their graphs and close the file without saving it. This will allow others to use the blank graph.

Extensions:

- Different types of food can be used instead of cookies.

- Students can create graphs of different types, such as a line graph or pie chart, using the original data on the cookies.

- Students can create problem questions based on the graph for others to answer.

- Students can poll classmates and graph other favorites, including ice cream, games to play, colors, etc.

COOKIE TASTE TEST RESULTS GRAPH

Red	
Blue	
Green	
Yellow	
Orange	

= a vote for that type of cookie

THE EYES HAVE IT!

Use the computer to introduce or review the concept of graphing.

Grade Level: 1–2

Duration: 40 minutes

Materials: Computer with paint program; printer; file of graph template on page 124; eye chart on page 125; small hand mirrors for students to use (optional).

Before the computer:

- The teacher should create the graph template on page 124 and save it in a file.

- The teacher should make a copy of the eye chart on page 125 for each student.

- Students should be familiar with the paint and draw tools and the stamp function in the paint program. Students should know how to print their work.

- Begin the activity by discussing the similarities and differences among people's appearances. Point out what color your eyes are and explain that your eye color might be similar to some students but different from others. Provide mirrors for students to determine their eye colors.

- Distribute the eye patterns and instruct students to color in the eye that is the same color as their eyes.

- As you call each color listed on the table, have students raise their eye patterns if their eyes are that color. Have a student help you count the eye patterns to determine how many students have each eye color. Record the data on the board and have students record the data at the bottom of their eye charts.

At the computer:

- Tell students that they are going to make a picture graph of their findings about eye color using the computer.

- Display the graph template in the paint program on the monitor.

- Explain to students that they are going to use an eye to represent each person who has that eye color.

- Ask students how many of them have blue eyes.

- Have a student draw one eye to represent each child who has blue eyes.

- Tell students that they will make their own picture graphs on the computer using their data.

- Have students print their graphs and then close the file without saving it. This will allow others to use the blank graph.

THE EYES HAVE IT! *(cont.)*

At the computer: *(cont)*

- Lead a class discussion about the graphs by asking questions similar to the following:

- Which eye color do most children have?

- Which eye color do the fewest number of children have?

- Are any of the eye colors equal in number? If yes, which colors?

- How many would you have to subtract from the most common eye color to make it equal to the second most common eye color?

- Would you have to add or subtract to make the number of children with blue eyes equal to the number of children with brown eyes?

- Can you think of any other ways to show the same information about the eyes?

Extensions:

- Have students create graphs for other topics such as: months of student birthdays, number of students who bring lunch, favorite colors, etc.

THE EYES HAVE IT! *(cont.)*

Our Eye Colors

Blue	Green	Brown	Gray

(👁) = number of students

THE EYES HAVE IT! *(cont.)*

Name _____

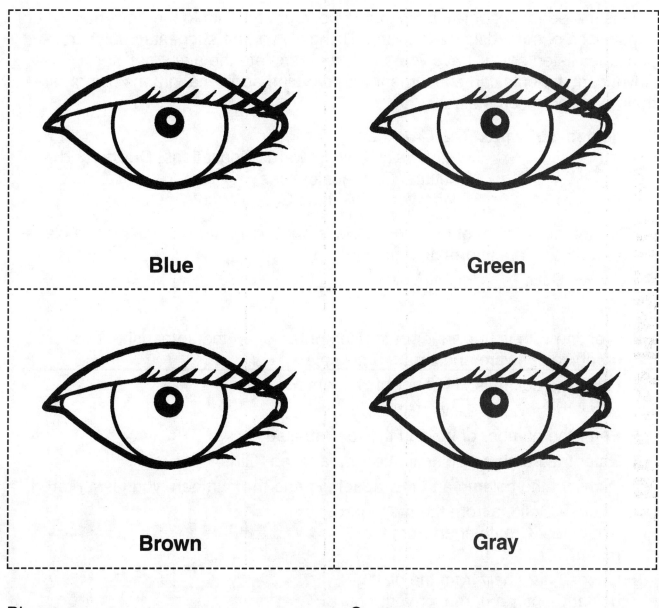

Blue	**Green**
Brown	**Gray**

Blue _____   Green _____

Brown _____   Gray _____

THE EYES HAVE IT! *(cont.)*

SOFTWARE CONNECTION:

This is the perfect opportunity to introduce your students to the powerful capabilities of spreadsheet software. Using any of the suggested software packages listed below, have your students complete the steps outlined. Advanced students can experiment with creating additional graphs using data they've collected on their own.

Suggested Software: *The Cruncher* by Davidson
Graphers by Lois Edwards Educational Design and Sunburst Communications
ClarisWorks by Claris Corporation (Apple)

1. Count the number of boys in the class and the number of girls in the class and record that information below.

    Boys_____

    Girls_____

2. Working with your partner at the computer, open the spreadsheet or graphing software and create a new file.

3. Label the columns: Number of Students

4. Label the rows: Boys Girls

5. Enter the number of boys in the row labelled "Boys."

6. Enter the number of girls in the row labelled "Girls."

7. Highlight the column and row headings and the numbers you just entered.

8. Choose Options from the menu bar and select Create chart from that menu.

9. Choose bar chart from the dialog box and enter a name for your chart.

10. Click on OK and position the chart where you want it to appear on the page.

11. Print the spreadsheet and chart, and quit the program.

12. Write your name on the print out and turn it in to your teacher.

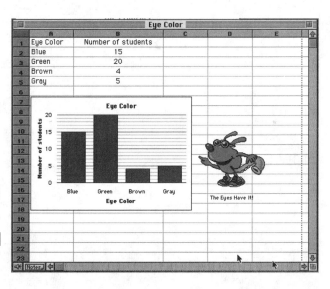

GRAPHING PIZZA

Create a pie chart to represent favorite pizza toppings.

Grade Level: 2–3

Duration: 30–40 minutes at the computer

Materials: Computer with paint program; copies of activity sheet on page 130

Before the computer:

- The teacher should make copies of the activity sheet for each student.

- Have students collect information about eight people's favorite pizza toppings the day before conducting this lesson. Limit the choices of pizza toppings to two or three, such as pepperoni, sausage, or cheese.

- Tell students they need to record people's answers on the activity sheet.

- Students should be familiar with the paint and draw tools in the paint program and should know how to print.

At the computer:

- Display a blank document in the paint program on the monitor.

- Explain to students that they will take the information they collected and make a pie chart showing what kinds of pizza toppings people like best.

- Ask eight students to share their own favorite pizza topping. Record this information on an overhead or blackboard.

- Show students how to draw a circle using the circle tool in the paint program.

- Show students how to divide the pie into eight equal slices using the line tool.

- Tell students that when making this pie chart, the number of people surveyed will equal the number of slices, in this case eight. The pie chart should resemble the picture on page 129.

GRAPHING PIZZA *(cont.)*

- Have students select three colors to represent the pizza toppings (i.e., red for pepperoni, brown for sausage, yellow for cheese).

- Ask students how many people liked pepperoni best, and how many slices should be colored red.

- Show students how to use the floodfill (paint bucket icon in most paint programs) to color the slices quickly.

- Continue with the other two toppings, coloring the slices the appropriate color.

- Have students create their own pie charts with the information they collected on the activity sheets.

- Have students print their pie charts and turn them in with the activity sheets.

Extensions:

- Students can complete the same activity with flavors of cake or ice cream.

- Students can pair up and compile their data into one pie chart.

- Students can compile class data and make a bar graph or line graph to illustrate findings.

PIE CHART FOR GRAPHING PIZZA

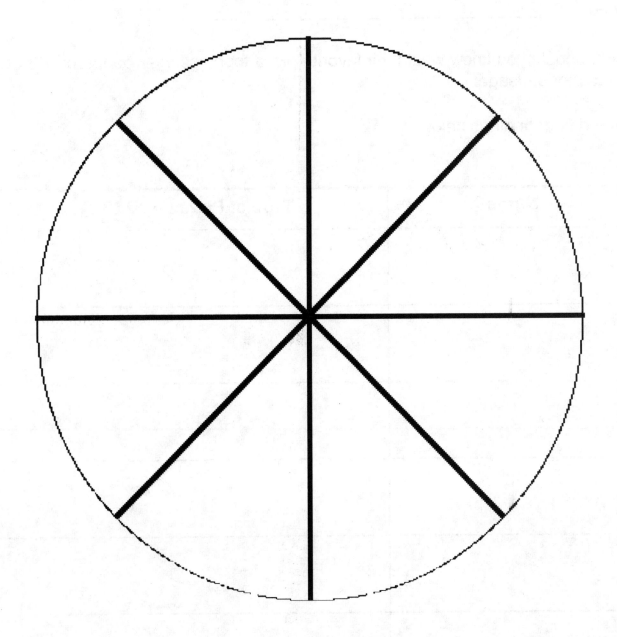

GRAPHING PIZZA *(cont.)*

Name _____

Ask 8 people you know what their favorite pizza toppings are: pepperoni, cheese, or sausage.

Record your findings below.

Name	Type of Pizza Liked Best
1.	
2.	
3.	
4.	
5.	
6.	
7.	
8.	

VENN DIAGRAM DRAWINGS

Collect data and create venn diagrams to display it.

Grade Level: 2–3

Duration: 20–30 minutes on the computer

Materials: Computer with paint software; printer; file with venn diagram on page 132

Before the computer:

- The teacher should introduce the concept of Venn diagrams to students and explain to them how they are created. The teacher should create and save a venn diagram file.

- Students should be familiar with the text tool, the draw tools, the stamp function, and how to edit the stamps.

- Students should know how to print their work.

At the compter:

- Display the file of the Venn diagram on the monitor.

- Tell students that they are going to make their own Venn diagrams on the computer.

- Have students pair up with partners.

- Ask students to describe themselves using adjectives (tall, brown skin, blue eyes, short hair, female, glasses, etc.). Have students record some of these traits and characteristics on a piece of paper.

- Demonstrate to students how to create a Venn diagram. Select two volunteers.

- Label the two circles with the volunteers' names. Type in a few of the characteristics they listed for themselves. When students share a characteristic, type the characteristic in the section where the two circles overlap.

- Explain to students that they could also illustrate this information in a more visual way. Show students how to edit stamps, for example, how to make the blue eye into a brown eye. Explain to students how to make a legend so that others will know what the pictures represent. See example on page 133.

- Pair students and have them collect data on each other and create a Venn diagram on the computer to show that data.

- Have students print the Venn diagram. Display these diagrams on a bulletin board.

- Remind students to close the file and not save the changes. This restores the template back to its original state.

- After all students have completed the Venn diagram, lead a class discussion on the similarities among the students.

Extensions:

- Students can make Venn diagrams with other types of data collected.

VENN DIAGRAM

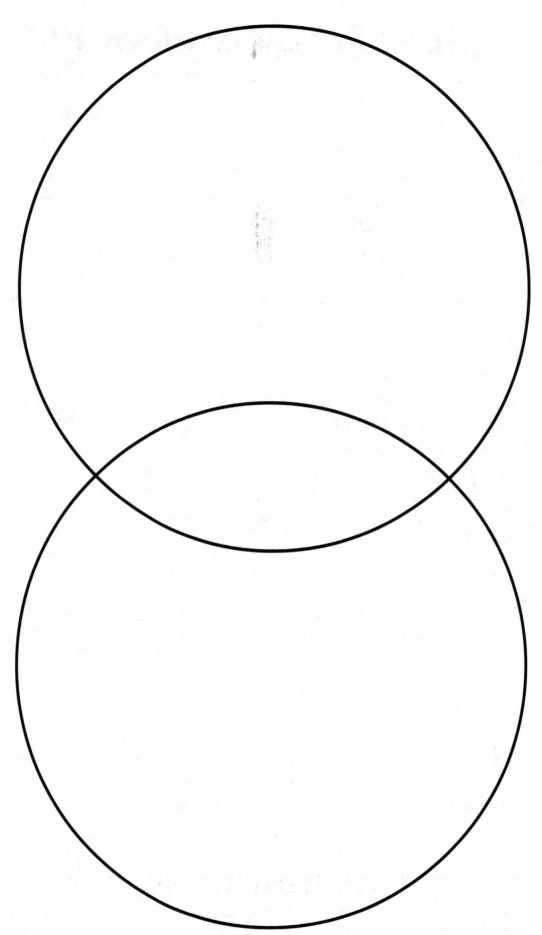

VENN DIAGRAM PAINT SAMPLES

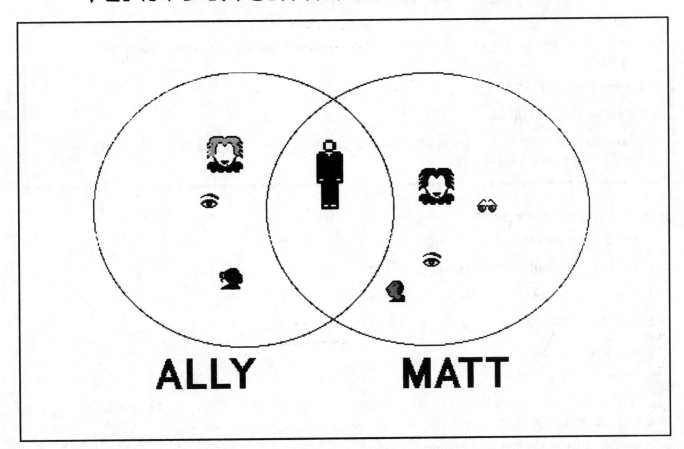

Legend

 = blond hair

 = brown hair

 = girl

 = boy

 =tall

 =short

 = glasses

 = blue eyes

 = brown eyes

INVESTIGATING GROUPS

Illustrate all the cominations that can be made using a specific number of objects.

Grade Level: 1–3

Duration: 20–30 minutes at the computer

Materials: Computer with paint software; sample paint files on page 135–139; copies of the activity sheet on page 140

Before using the computer:

- The teacher should create the paint files on page 135–139.

- The teacher should also make a copy of the activity sheet for each student.

- Students should know how to drag and drop objects on the screen.

- Students should be familiar with the print function.

At the computer:

- Display the paint file on the monitor.

- Tell students that they will move pictures around on the computer screen to create a new arrangement of pictures.

- Show students the first set of pictures in the file.

- Ask students to predict how many different ways they can arrange these pictures.

- Have students create a different arrangement of the pictures from the first set. Continue until all possibilities are exhausted.

- Ask students to count how many different groupings they were able to make and to record this number on their activity sheet.

- Have students continue the activity independently until all of the sets are completed.

- Be sure that students print out their screens to turn in with the activity sheets.

- Have students identify patterns among the combinations.

Extensions:

- More or less pictures can be used in the file, depending on students' level of understanding.

INVESTIGATING GROUPS *(cont.)*

SAMPLE PAINT FILES

How many ways can you arrange these pictures?

next slide

INVESTIGATING GROUPS *(cont.)*

SAMPLE PAINT FILES

How many ways can you arrange these pictures?

next slide

INVESTIGATING GROUPS *(cont.)*

SAMPLE PAINT FILES

How many ways can you arrange these pictures?

next slide

INVESTIGATING GROUPS *(cont.)*

SAMPLE PAINT FILES

How many ways can you arrange these pictures?

back to page 1

INVESTIGATING GROUPS *(cont.)*

SAMPLE PAINT FILES

How many ways can you arrange these pictures?

next slide

INVESTIGATING GROUPS *(cont.)*

Name _____

1. Set #1:

   How many different combinations did you find? _____

2. Set #2:

   How many different combinations did you find? _____

3. Set #3:

   How many different combinations did you find? _____

4. Set #4:

   How many different combinations did you find? _____

5. Set #5:

   How many different combinations did you find? _____

   Can you see any kind of pattern? Describe it.

   _____

   _____

   _____

   _____

   _____

MATH LETTERS

Write letters to math pen pals explaining a particular math concept.

Grade Level: 2–3

Duration: 20–30 minutes at the computer

Materials: Computer with word processing software; printer; another class of students

Before using the computer:

- The teacher should discuss with students what they have learned in math this year and which lesson they enjoyed the most. The teacher can have the students brainstorm some of their favorite lessons to generate ideas for their pen pal letters.

- The teacher should arrange with another class to be math pen pals, with the topic of the letters being math concepts.

- Students should be familiar with how to enter letters and numbers into a word processing program.

- Students should know how to print their work.

At the computer:

- Display a blank document in the word processing program on the monitor.

- Tell students they are going to write letters to their pen pals explaining their favorite math activities or concepts.

- Show students how to use the word processing software to write their letters. Each letter should include the lesson, the math skill learned, and why this lesson is the student's favorite.

- Explain to students that the letters do not have to be very long, but should be detailed enough so that their pen pal will understand what the lesson was and how to do the math.

- Have students write their letters.

- Ask students to pair up and respond to each other's letters as editors, checking for spelling and grammar conventions and determining if the math is clearly explained. An older student or assistant may need to help edit some of the letters.

- Have students save the file and print the letter.

- Tell students that you will collect and send the letters.

- Continue the pen pal letter writing throughout the school year, each time writing about a math related concept.

Extensions:

- Students can collect data about the kinds of math concepts being shared with pen pals. What is the class favorite? What concept is the class runner-up? What concept does the class want to learn more about?

MATH JOURNALS

Compile entries from student math journals.

Grade Level: 2–3

Duration: 15–20 minutes at the computer each time an entry is entered

Materials: Computer with word processing software

Before using the computer:

- The teacher should have students keep a written journal where they regularly write about math concepts. Students can explain the math concept, write steps for solving problems, explain how answers were achieved, or tell about any difficulties they encountered.

- Students should know how to enter letters and numbers into the word processing program and how to print.

At the computer:

- Display a blank word processing document on the monitor.

- Explain to students that they will select one of their journal entries to type into the computer.

- Show students how to enter the journal entry in the word processing program.

- Show students how to edit their journal for reability and clarity. Students can pair up to act as editors for each other's journal entry. An older student or teacher's assistant may be needed to help edit the journal entries.

- Tell students to save their entries in a file and print their documents.

- These printed entries can be compiled into a Class Math Journal. This can be displayed at Open House for parents to read.

Extensions:

- Students can type problems for others to solve in their journals.

SOFTWARE DESCRIPTIONS

Several types of software are used as the basis for the lessons in this book. The following descriptions explain the basic functions of each type of software and give examples. These definitions do not explain how specific software operates or provide ordering information on a particular package.

Paint and Draw Software

Paint and draw software enables the user to create drawings and paintings on the computer screen. Many of the paint and draw tools mimic their physical counterparts, such as the pencil tool or freeform tool which allows you to draw lines as you would with a pencil, the paintbrush tool which is similar to a paintbrush, and the stamp function which is like a rubber stamp. The paint and draw software, however, has additional tools that are not available elsewhere. For example, the straight line tool draws a straight line; the shape tools create that particular shape of different sizes, and the floodfill (paint bucket) fills in a shape completely with a designated color or pattern.

Paint files can be saved or printed just as text files are. Clip art can be created in paint software and used in other types of documents or software such as multimedia slide shows or stories that have been word processed.

There are many different software packages on the market, some more complex than others. Be sure to use a paint and draw program appropriate for students' skills and abilities.

Spreadsheet Software

Spreadsheet software enables the user to enter numbers and formulas into a grid or chart style format. Formulas automatically perform the calculation on the entered numbers. This provides the user with answers quickly and accurately. Many spreadsheet programs also have a graphing function that works with a spreadsheet to create graphic representations of data.

Graphing Software

Graphing software is often included in other types of software such as word processing programs, spreadsheet programs, or integrated packages. The graphing software utilizes the entered numbers or data to create graphical representations of the data in various forms. Most graphing software can create professional looking bar charts, 3-D bar charts, pie charts and 3-D pie charts. Colors can be added to make the charts easy to read.

Database Software

Database software enables the user to enter data collected on a particular topic into a file that has been formatted in a particular way. Fields or categories of data within the topic must be selected and entered into the database file. Data is entered into each field and then saved to create a record within the database. A collection of records is a file. When the database is complete, information about the data can be obtained by having the computer search the database or sort the files looking for specific information. The database user can ask questions formated in a particular way to access information in the database. The user should consult the instruction manual to learn the format for queries.

SOFTWARE DESCRIPTIONS *(cont.)*

Database Software *(cont.)*

Spreadsheet software that is compatible with a database package can have cells that access certain fields in the database files and automatically update the figures in the fields as they are changed in the database. The spreadsheet then automatically performs required calculations on the new figures.

Multimedia Authoring Software

This type of software is called authoring software because it allows the user to create or author a package. Multimedia refers to combining different types of media or communication such as text, sound, animation, video, and graphics. Most of these packages use the card or slide show format. The user creates cards or slides that are connected together.

There are mainly two types of multimedia authoring software—linear and non-linear. Linear automatically connects slides to each other in the order in which they were created. When the slide is completed, the user clicks on the mouse to move to the next slide. Slides can not be taken out of order but they can be skipped or hidden in most packages. Earlier versions of this type of software did not always allow sound or animation to be included, but newer versions have these features.

Non-linear authoring software allows the user to move through slides in any order or move back to slides already shown through the creation of hyper buttons or hot buttons. These buttons generally are multi-functional and allow the user to choose the function of the button, including which slide to go to next. This type of multimedia software is newer and usually allows the user more flexibility of use. Graphics and sound brought in from various sources can be added to the slides, along with animation and videos.

Word Processing Software

Word processing software enables the user to enter text by typing on the keyboard. The entered text can be easily changed and edited. Most word processing programs offer a spell check feature that automatically searches out the misspelled words and typos and assists with corrections. Many word processing programs also offer a grammar check feature that checks sentence structure, word usage, and punctuation.

Integrated Packages

Integrated packages are software programs that combine some of the above listed software programs. These packages provide the user with word processing, spreadsheet, database, and graphing software that is compatible and easy to use. Users can move data between the various programs. For example, information entered in a database can also be entered as a text document in a word processing program. Spreadsheets can automatically update the data entered in a database and perform the required calculations.